C000119004

YOU BURY ME

by Ahlam

Copyright © 2023 by Ahlam
Photography by Rebecca Need-Menear
Design by madeby.DO
All Rights Reserved

YOU BURY ME is fully protected under the copyright laws of the British Commonwealth, including Canada, the United States of America, and all other countries of the Copyright Union. All rights, including professional and amateur stage productions, recitation, lecturing, public reading, motion picture, radio broadcasting, television, online/digital production, and the rights of translation into foreign languages are strictly reserved.

ISBN 978-0-573-13381-7

concordtheatricals.co.uk
concordtheatricals.com

FOR AMATEUR PRODUCTION ENQUIRIES

UNITED KINGDOM AND WORLD
EXCLUDING NORTH AMERICA
licensing@concordtheatricals.co.uk
020-7054-7298

Each title is subject to availability from Concord Theatricals, depending upon country of performance.

CAUTION: Professional and amateur producers are hereby warned that *YOU BURY ME* is subject to a licensing fee. The purchase, renting, lending or use of this book does not constitute a licence to perform this title(s), which licence must be obtained from the appropriate agent prior to any performance. Performance of this title(s) without a licence is a violation of copyright law and may subject the producer and/or presenter of such performances to penalties. Both amateurs and professionals considering a production are strongly advised to apply to the appropriate agent before starting rehearsals, advertising, or booking a theatre. A licensing fee must be paid whether the title is presented for charity or gain and whether or not admission is charged.

This work is published by Samuel French, an imprint of Concord Theatricals Ltd.

Please direct all Professional Rights enquiries to Concord Theatricals Ltd. Aldwych House, 71-91 Aldwych, London, WC2B 4HN.

No one shall make any changes in this title for the purpose of production. No part of this book may be reproduced, stored in a retrieval system, scanned, uploaded, or transmitted in any form, by any means, now known or yet to be invented, including mechanical, electronic, digital, photocopying, recording, videotaping, or otherwise, without the prior written permission of the publisher. No one shall share this title, or part of this title, to any social media or file hosting websites.

The moral right of Ahlam to be identified as author of this work has been asserted in accordance with Section 77 of the Copyright, Designs and Patents Act 1988.

USE OF COPYRIGHTED MUSIC

A licence issued by Concord Theatricals to perform this play does not include permission to use the incidental music specified in this publication. In the United Kingdom: Where the place of performance is already licensed by the PERFORMING RIGHT SOCIETY (PRS) a return of the music used must be made to them. If the place of performance is not so licensed then application should be made to PRS for Music (www.prsformusic.com). A separate and additional licence from PHONOGRAPHIC PERFORMANCE LTD (www.ppluk.com) may be needed whenever commercial recordings are used. Outside the United Kingdom: Please contact the appropriate music licensing authority in your territory for the rights to any incidental music.

USE OF COPYRIGHTED THIRD-PARTY MATERIALS

Licensees are solely responsible for obtaining formal written permission from copyright owners to use copyrighted third-party materials (e.g., artworks, logos) in the performance of this play and are strongly cautioned to do so. If no such permission is obtained by the licensee, then the licensee must use only original materials that the licensee owns and controls. Licensees are solely responsible and liable for clearances of all third-party copyrighted materials, and shall indemnify the copyright owners of the play(s) and their licensing agent, Concord Theatricals Ltd., against any costs, expenses, losses and liabilities arising from the use of such copyrighted third-party materials by licensees.

IMPORTANT BILLING AND CREDIT REQUIREMENTS

If you have obtained performance rights to this title, please refer to your licensing agreement for important billing and credit requirements.

YOU BURY ME was co-produced by Paines Plough, The Women's Prize for Playwriting, 45North, The Royal Lyceum Theatre Edinburgh and the Orange Tree Theatre, in association with Bristol Old Vic. It was first performed on 24th February 2023. The cast was as follows:

RAFIK. . . . . Nezar Alderazi
TAMER. . . . . Moe Bar-El
OSMAN. . . . . Tarrick Benham
ALIA. . . . . Hanna Khogali
LINA. . . . . Eleanor Nawal
MAYA. . . . . .Yasemin Özdemir

Writer – Ahlam
Director – Katie Posner
Designer – Sara Perks
Lighting Designer – Aideen Malone
Composer – Kareem Samara
Sound Designer – Adam P McCready
Movement Director – Annie-Lunnette Deakin-Foster
Casting Director – Jacob Sparrow
Assistant Director – Riwa Saab
Intimacy Director – Robbie Taylor Hunt
Production Manager – Ryan Funnell
Company Stage Manager – Lois Sime
Assistant Stage Manager – Charlotte Smith-Barker
Technical Stage Manager – Simon Perkins
Lighting Programmer (Bristol Old Vic)/Relighter (Edinburgh Lyceum) – Matthew Carnazza
Costume Supervisor – Manuela Fleming

With thanks to:
Indhu Rubasingham, Nina Steiger, Sarah Dickenson, Dennis Kelly, Tanya Agarwal, Katie Austin, Phillippe Cato, Ellie Claughton, Holly Gladwell, Lauren Hamilton, Christabel Holmes, Jesse Jones and Ellen Larson.

This play has had various pockets of support through its writing and development. Thank you to the various organisations that offered space and time over the years. Thanks to the festivals and theatres that platformed the play through various readings. Thank you to all the actors that have brought these characters to life in these developments and readings. Thank you to Sophie Moniram who championed the script from draft one and never ceased to believe in it. Thank you to the playwrights that took time to read, feedback and mentor me through the process of writing draft after draft. And finally thank you to my friends and family who supported me through meltdowns when I thought the script was utter shit. Unfortunately I cannot name most of the people or organisations in order to maintain my anonymity but I would like to say a big thank you to all anyway, without your support this script would not exist.

CAST

NEZAR ALDERAZI | RAFIK
Nezar Alderazi trained as an actor at AUC in Egypt and at East 15 Acting School in the UK.

Theatre includes: *Occupational Hazards* (Hampstead Theatre); *The Outsider* (The Coronet Theatre); *Waiting for Godot* (Falaki Theatre, Egypt).

Television includes: *The Looming Tower, Casualty, The B@it.*

Film includes: *The Mauritanian, David French is a Piece of Shit and I Want Him Dead.*

Radio includes: *The Sandman: Act 2, Moby Dick, Arabian Nights Parts 1 & 2.*

MOE BAR-EL | TAMER
Moe is an Olivier-award nominated actor originally from Iran.

Theatre includes: *The Jungle* (West End); *Every Day I Make Greatness Happen* (Hampstead Theatre); *Welcome to Iran* (Theatre Royal Stratford East); *Lockdown and All That/The Monster Inside* (Tara Theatre); *Moormaid* (Arcola Theatre); *Punk Rock* (Courtyard Theatre); *Awkward Silence* (Sadler's Wells).

Television includes: *The Peripheral* (Amazon Prime); *Tehran* and *Invasion* (Apple TV); *Dinner with the Parents* (Amazon Freevee); *Honour* and *Count Abdulla* (ITV); *The Bureau* (Canal+), *Snatch* (Crackle); *PhoneShop* (Channel 4); *Black Mirror* (Netflix); *Tyrant* (FX).

Film includes: *Femme, Zero, Austenland, Mitra.*

TARRICK BENHAM | OSMAN
Tarrick trained at The Arts Educational Schools London.

Theatre includes: *New Voices for a New World* (Oxford Playhouse); *Demonstration* (Southwark Playhouse); *White Horses* (Northern Stage, Newcastle); *Dr Blighty* (Brighton Dome); *Mindwalking* (UK tour); *Heart* (UK tour); *We Gamble Responsibly* (Pleasance Theatre, London); *The Emperor's Lost Gem* (Luton Arts Centre); *Casino Royale* (Secret Cinema); *A Gym Thing* (Edinburgh Festival Fringe); *7 Jewish Children* (Brighton Festival).

Television includes: *Snatch, EastEnders, The Royals, Drifters, Holby City, Coronation Street, Hollyoaks, Doctors.*

Film includes: *Mission: Impossible - Rogue Nation, Swimming with Men, Involuntary Activist, The River, For the Best, Domestik, Mankurt.*

Radio includes: *Pride & Prejudice*

HANNA KHOGALI | ALIA

Hanna trained at Guildford School of Acting.

Theatre includes: *You Bury Me* (Paines Plough); *Britannicus* (Lyric Hammersmith); *71 Coltman Street* (Hull Truck); *Brief Encounter* (The Watermill); *Once* (UK tour); *Swallows and Amazons* (York Theatre Royal); *Moll Flanders* (Mercury Theatre); *Good Fit* (Southwark Playhouse); *The Lost Ones* (Bush Theatre); *The Collection* (The Wallace Collection); *Rags* (Hope Mill – UK Premiere); *Broken Wings* (The Other Palace) and *Daisy Pulls it Off* (Charing Cross Theatre).

ELEANOR NAWAL | LINA

Eleanor Nawal is a British Egyptian actor and writer from London.

Theatre includes: *Sherlock in Homes* and *Sherlock in Homes 2* (Bristol Old Vic/Wardrobe Theatre); *Polly: the Heartbreak Opera* (Sharp Teeth Theatre, UK tour); *Underwater Love* (Futures Theatre).

Television includes: *Launderette* (BBC pilot); *A Whole Lifetime* (BBC/Netflix); *The Full Monty* (Disney+); *Somewhere Boy* (Channel 4); *Pls Like* (BBC); *The Alienist* (Paramount); *Urban Myths* (Sky).

YASEMIN ÖZDEMIR | MAYA

Yasemin trained at the Royal Welsh College of Music & Drama, graduating in 2020.

Theatre includes: *Angel* – Offies Award nomination (UK tour); *Dance to the Bone* (Sherman Theatre); *Living Newspaper* (The Royal Court); *We Need to Talk About Grief* (Donmar Warehouse); *Romeo & Juliet* (New Theatre Cardiff/Theatr Clwyd); *Pride and Prejudice* (Artistic License).

Television includes: *A Spy Among Friends* (ITV); *Vandullz* (BBC).

Film includes: *Yummy Mummy, Patrick*.

Radio and voice over credits include: *With Great Pleasure: Michael Rosen* and *English Rose* (BBC Radio 4); *In Search of Captain Cat* (BBC Radio Wales) and *Warhammer 40,000: Darktide* (Fatshark/Molinaire).

Yasemin is a highly skilled physical actress with a passion for stage combat. She was a part of the fighting cohort for the epic action film *Lady of Heaven*.

CREATIVE

AHLAM | WRITER

Ahlam moved around a lot as a child. She has lived in Germany, Singapore, Kenya, Venezuela, Turkey and the UK. She initially studied theatre in Egypt, where she created work combining elements of classical Greek Theatre and surrealism with contemporary dance, based on her heartbreak. Her interest in text-based theatre was forced upon her in true British tradition, when she was asked to write a reimagining of Indiana Jones to take to the Edinburgh Fringe. Luckily, it turns out she quite likes writing. Ahlam is a dreamer. Ahlam dreams of revolution. Ahlam dreams of the emancipatory power of day-dreaming. Ahlam dreams of big ensemble theatre with giant sets. Ahlam dreams of pistachio-crusted salmon she ate once in Sicily. Ahlam dreams of love. *You Bury Me* isn't the first play she's written and it won't be her last.

KATIE POSNER | DIRECTOR

Katie Posner (she/her) joined Paines Plough as Joint Artistic Director with Charlotte Bennett in August 2019. Katie has most recently directed - *Hungry* for Soho Theatre/ Roundabout Edinburgh, *Really Big and Really Loud*, *Black Love* (Co-Director for Roundabout) and *You Bury Me* staged reading for the Edinburgh International Festival (Paines Plough/Ellie Keel Productions/45 North).

Katie is an experienced and award-winning director. She has worked across a wide variety of productions both overseas and on national tours, including multiple productions with York Theatre Royal and Pilot Theatre with whom she was Associate Director from 2009 until 2017. Her work encompasses both intimate pieces of new writing and larger-scale community pieces. In 2019 Katie received a UK Theatre Award nomination as Best Director with her production of *My Mother Said I Never Should* at Theatre By The Lake.

Productions include: *My Mother Said I Never Should* (Theatre By The Lake); *Mold Riots* (Theatr Clwyd); *The Seven Ages Of Patience* (Kiln Theatre); *Swallows & Amazons* (Storyhouse), *Babe* (Mercury Theatre); *Playing Up* (NYT); *Finding Nana* (New Perspectives); *Made In India* (Tamasha/Belgrade/Pilot); Everything Is Possible: *The York Suffragettes*, *End Of Desire* (York Theatre Royal); *The Season Ticket* (Northern Stage); *A View From Islington North* (Out Of Joint); *In Fog And Falling Snow* (National Railway Museum); *Running On The Cracks* (Tron Theatre); *York Mystery Plays* (Museum Gardens York); *Blackbird, Ghost Town, Clocking In, A Restless Place* (Pilot Theatre).

SARA PERKS | DESIGNER

Sara Perks holds a BA Hons in Drama & Theatre Studies and trained in Theatre Design at Bristol Old Vic Theatre School. She was previously Head of Design for Shakespeare's Rose Theatre (York and Blenheim), designing *Macbeth*, *A Midsummer Night's Dream*, *Twelfth Night* and *Hamlet*, as well as managing the design departments for eight concurrent productions. She has also held the roles of Associate Artist at Mercury Theatre, Colchester (having designed over 35 shows there) and Associate Designer with English Touring Theatre.

She has designed over 275 productions to date for every type of venue and genre. Recent work includes: *Mind Mangler* (UK tour/West End, Mischief Theatre); *Around the World in 80 Days* (UK tour, York Theatre Royal/Tilted Wig); *71 Coltman Street* (Hull Truck); *Now Is Good* (Storyhouse, Chester); *Good Luck, Studio* (Mischief Theatre/Mercury); *Footloose!* (International Tour, Selladoor); *The Rise and Fall of Little Voice* (UK tour, Aria). She has been nominated for both Broadway World Awards (Set Design and Costume Design) and a WhatsOnStage Award (Set Design) for *American Idiot*, an Offie for *Oranges and Elephants*, and holds an Edinburgh Fringe First, The John Elvery Theatre Design Award, and a Vision Design (Costume) Award from the BBC.

AIDEEN MALONE | LIGHTING DESIGNER

Credits include: *Lemons Lemons Lemons Lemons Lemons* (West End); *The Clothes They Stood Up* (Nottingham Playhouse); *Wonder Boy* (Bristol Old Vic); *Hamlet* (Young Vic); *Running With Lions* (Lyric Hammersmith); *A Kind Of People* (Royal Court); *Now Is Good* (Storyhouse); *Carousel* (Regents Park); *Death of a Salesman* (Young Vic & Piccadilly); *Old Bridge* (Bush); *A Monster Calls* (Old Vic & Bristol Old Vic); *Brighton Rock* (York Theatre Royal); *La Strada* (The Other Palace); *Jane Eyre*; *Peter Pan* (National Theatre); *Worst Witch* (Vaudeville); *Hetty Feather* (Duke of York); *The Strange Tale of Stan Laurel* and *Charlie Chaplin* (Told By An Idiot); *A Raisin in the Sun*, *Talent* (Sheffield Theatres); *Kaash*, *Outwitting The Devil* (Aram Khan Co.).

KAREEM SAMARA | COMPOSER

Kareem Samara is a musician and composer from London. A strong believer in collaboration, he works with a wide variety of poets, writers and musicians across many disciplines in Europe, the USA and the Middle East. His work for theatre combines traditional Arab and western acoustic instruments along with electronics, creating a unique soundscape and performance.

Productions as composer include: *Hakawatis: Women of the Arabian Nights* (Shakespeare's Globe); *A History of Water in the Middle East* (Royal Court Theatre); *The Chronicles of Majnoon Leila* (Gate Theatre); *Wipe These Tears* (Camden People's Theatre).

ADAM P MCCREADY | SOUND DESIGNER

Adam P McCready is a sound designer, composer, sound recordist and performer of neo-ambient electronica. Adam has created sound designs and music scores for theatre, dance productions, radio and audio dramas, audiobooks, podcast series, and film. He has also devised several multi-speaker, interactive sound installations for galleries and museums. His work focuses on creating soundscapes that combine ambiences with music and digitally manipulated sound recordings.

Adam is also a trustee of Can't Sit Still Theatre and an associate artist with 1623 Theatre and Little Pixie Productions.

Socials and Bandcamp @AdamPMcCready

JACOB SPARROW | CASTING DIRECTOR

Theatre includes: *A Sudden Violent Burst of Rain, Half-Empty Glasses, The Ultimate Pickle, Hungry* (Paines Plough); *Orlando* (West End); *Oklahoma!* (Young Vic/West End), *As You Like It* (Soho Place); *Hedwig and the Angry Inch* (Leeds/HOME Manchester); *Anna Karenina, Much Ado About Nothing* (Sheffield Crucible); *Curious Incident of the Dog in the Night-Time* (2021 tour); *Jitney* (Old Vic/Headlong/Leeds Playhouse), *Burn It Down* (Theatre Royal Stratford East); *Once On This Island, Carousel, Our Town* (Regents Park), *LOVE, Faith, Hope and Charity* (Dorfman/European tours); *The Book Thief* (Bolton Octagon); *Wuthering Heights* (Wise Children); *The Good Person of Szechwan* (ETT); *Village Idiot* (Nottingham Playhouse); *Black Love* (Kiln Theatre); *Perspectives* (New Views); *City of Angels* (West End); *Hadestown, Pericles, Follies, Amadeus* (all Olivier Theatre); *LOVE* (Dorfman/International Tour/Film); *Queer Season, Rutherford and Son, Faith Hope and Charity, Mr Gum, Downstate* (National Theatre).

Jacob worked in the NT Casting Department from 2015 to 2019 before becoming a freelance Casting Director. Prior to working at the National Theatre, Jacob worked with Pippa Ailion Casting and Telsey and Company in New York, as well as alongside James Orange.

ANNIE-LUNNETTE DEAKIN-FOSTER | MOVEMENT DIRECTOR

Annie-Lunnette Deakin-Foster is a London based Movement Director and Choreographer.

Theatre includes: *Pop Music, You Stupid Darkness!, On The Other Hand We're Happy, Daughterhood, Dexter and Winter's Detective Agency* (Paines Plough); *Lemons Lemons Lemons Lemons Lemons, Cock* (West End); *The Flood* (Queen's Theatre); *The Famous Five* (Chichester/Theatr Clwyd); *Heart* (Minetta Lane Theatre, New York); *Romeo & Juliet, Little Women* (Grosvenor Park Open Air Theatre); *An Octoroon* (Abbey Theatre); *Mum* (Soho Theatre/Theatre Royal Plymouth); *Rockets and Blue Lights* (National Theatre); *Robin Hood, Beauty And The Beast, The Panto That Nearly Never Was, Pavilion* (Theatr Clwyd); *Black Victorians* (UK tour); *Overflow, Chiaroscuro* (The Bush); *The Bee in Me, Aesop's Fables, Grimm Tales* (Unicorn); *The Last Noel* (Arts at the Old Fire Station/ UK tour); *Jericho's Rose* (The Hope & Anchor); *The Court Must Have a Queen* (Hampton Court Palace); *These Bridges* (National Theatre Connections/The Bush); *The Little Match Girl, Other Happier Tales* (Shakespeare's Globe/UK tour); *The Dark Room* (Theatre503).

RIWA SAAB | ASSISTANT DIRECTOR

Riwa Saab is a multidisciplinary artist. She graduated from Guildhall School of Music and Drama. Her original work has been performed at the Barbican and Soho Theatre.

As a Sound Designer she has worked on *Babel* (Camden People's Theatre); *Butterflies of Life* (Jermyn Street Theatre); *A Guest* (Vault Festival); *Redbrick* (Jermyn Street Theatre). As an associate sound designer she has worked on *Human Nurture* (Theatre Centre, UK Tour). She has produced work with Shubbak Festival and the Royal Court. *You Bury Me* is her first role as an assistant director.

ROBBIE TAYLOR HUNT | INTIMACY DIRECTOR

Robbie Taylor Hunt (he/him) is an Intimacy Director & Coordinator, and theatre-maker.

Theatre includes: *Animal* (Park Theatre/UK tour); *Fatal Attraction* (UK tour); *Foxes* (Theatre503, Seven Dials Playhouse); *Yes So I Said Yes* (Finborough Theatre); *Very Special Guest Star* (Omnibus Theatre); *Passionfruit* (New Diorama). Television includes: *Mary & George, You, Get Millie Black, Big Boys, The Bastard Son and The Devil Himself, The Wheel of Time, Belgravia, Domina, Somewhere Boy, Liaison.* Film includes: *Femme, Red White and Royal Blue, Pearl, Matriarch.*

His theatre-making credits include: *Lesbian Space Crime* (Soho Theatre); *Tuna* (UK tour); *Eris* (Bunker); *how we love* (Arcola, Theatre Peckham).

RYAN FUNNELL | PRODUCTION MANAGER
Production management includes: *Reasons You Should(n't) Love Me* (Paines Plough/UK tour); Longborough Festival Opera Season 2023, *The Wellspring* (Royal & Derngate Theatre/UK tour); *Shakespeariance* (DHP/Hampton Court Palace); *Mum* (Playground Theatre London); *The Talented Mr. Ripley* (The Faction Theatre Company/UK tour); *Ages of the Moon, The Permanent Way* (DHP/Vaults London).
Ryan is also a Theatre Consultant with Stage Right Theatre Consultants Ltd, and was previously Head of Technical & Facilities at Wilton's Music Hall. He studied Design & Technical Theatre Arts at Middlesex University.

LOIS SIME | COMPANY STAGE MANAGER
Lois trained at Guildhall School of Music and Drama, specialising in stage management. Credits include: *Old Bridge* (Bush Theatre); *Game of Love and Chance* (Arcola Theatre) and *Clybourne Park* (The Park).

CHARLOTTE SMITH-BARKER | ASSISTANT STAGE MANAGER
Charlotte studied English Literature and Film at Aberystwyth University and Malmö University in Sweden. Upon graduating in 2018, she completed the association of British Theatre Technicians Bronze Award. Theatre includes: *The Ultimate Pickle, A Sudden Violent Burst of Rain, Half-Empty Glasses* (Paines Plough); *The Catherine Tate Show* (West End); *One Woman Show* (West End); *Cages* (Riverside Studios); *Mary* (Hampstead Theatre); *Clybourne Park* (Park Theatre); *Soho Cinders* (Charing Cross Theatre); *The Sweet Science of Bruising* (Wilton's Music Hall)

SIMON PERKINS | TECHNICAL STAGE MANAGER
Theatre includes: *Chimerica, Cinderella* (Theatre Royal Stratford East); *Running With Lions* (Lyric Hammersmith); *Look At Me Don't Look At Me, Oh Mother, Snow White & Rose Red, Two Man Show, We Want You To Watch* (RashDash); *The End of Eddy, Told By An Idiot* (Unicorn Theatre); *Get Happy, Complicité, I'll Take You To Mrs Cole!* (Royal & Derngate); *The Remains of the Day, Made in China* (Super Duper Close Up); *Beyond Caring* (Alexander Zeldin); *Romeo & Juliet* (Shakespeare's Globe); *Misty, Black Lives/Black Words* (Bush Theatre); *Grounded* (The Gate); *Am I Dead Yet?* (Unlimited).

MATTHEW CARNAZZA | LIGHTING PROGRAMMER (BRISTOL OLD VIC)/ RELIGHTER (EDINBURGH LYCEUM)

Theatre credits as lighting designer include: *Cinderella* (UK Tour); *The Girl With The Tale* (Dance City); *Dance Nation* (Omnibus Theatre); *122 Love Stories* (Harrogate Theatre); *Against* (ALRA); *The Producers* (Bridewell Theatre); *The Collective* (Dance City/UK tour); *Syndrome* (Tristan Bates Theatre); *Vernon God Little* (Stratford Circus); *Our House* (Italia Conti); *Tutu Trouble* (Fairfield Halls); *JV2* (Sadler's Wells/UK tour); *Duchess of Malfi* (Rose Theatre).

Theatre credits as associate lighting designer or programmer include: *Here* (Southwark Playhouse); *The Clothes They Stood Up In* (Nottingham Playhouse); *ALiCE* (JVH.o.m.e/UK tour); *Mikado* (UK tour); *Saturn Returns* (Riley Theatre); *Infinite Ways Home* (UK tour).

MANUELA FLEMING | COSTUME SUPERVISOR

Manuela is a costume supervisor and wardrobe manager from Bristol. Wardrobe Manager credits include: *The Nutcracker, Dr Semmelweis* (Bristol Old Vic); *Ballet Black at 20: Double Bill* (UK tour); *Cinderella* (Theatre Royal Bath); *The Hooley* (Giffords Circus/UK tour).

Costume Supervisor credits include: *Fools Delight* (Fools Delight Circus); *Venus and Adonis* (Blackheath Halls Opera). Manuela is also an emerging designer for dance, circus and theatre.

Design credits include: *Don't Mind Me* (Sadler's Wells); *Journey South, The Secret* (Laban Theatre).

As Design Associate: *Tamerlano* (Cambridge Handel Opera Company).

As Design Assistant: *Venus and Adonis* (Blackheath Halls Opera); *The Magic Flute* (Waterperry Opera Company).

Paines Plough

Paines Plough is the national theatre of new plays. A touring company dedicated entirely to developing and producing exceptional new writing, the work we create connects with artists and communities across the UK.

"The lifeblood of the UK's theatre ecosystem." The Guardian

Since 1974 Paines Plough has worked with over 300 world renowned playwrights including James Graham, Sarah Kane, Dennis Kelly, Kae Tempest, Vinay Patel, Mike Bartlett, Sam Steiner, Elinor Cook and Zia Ahmed.

Our plays are nationally identified and locally heard. We tour to over 40 places a year and are committed to bringing work to communities who might not otherwise have the opportunity to experience much new writing or theatre. We reach over 30,000 people annually from Cornwall to the Orkney Islands, in village halls, off-Broadway and in our own pop-up theatre Roundabout; a state of the art, in the round auditorium which travels the length and breadth of the country.

"That noble company Paines Plough, de facto national theatre of new writing." The Telegraph

Furthering our reach beyond theatre walls, our audio app *Come to Where I'm From* hosts 180 original mini plays about home and our digital projects connect with audiences via WhatsApp, phone, email and even by post.

Wherever you are, you can experience a Paines Plough production.

"I think some theatre just saved my life." @kate_clement on Twitter

Paines Plough

Joint Artistic Directors & CEOs	Charlotte Bennett & Katie Posner
Executive Director	Jodie Gilliam
Producer	Ellie Fitz-Gerald
Digital Producer	Nick Virk
Marketing and Audience Development Manager	Manwah Siu
Administrator	Mrinmoyee Roy
The Big Room Playwright Fellow	Mufaro Makubika
Press Representative	Bread and Butter PR

Board of Directors
Kim Grant (Chair), Ankur Bahl, Corey Campbell, Asma Hussain, Tarek Iskander, Olivier Pierre-Noël, Carolyn Saunders and Laura Wade

Paines Plough Limited is a company limited by guarantee and a registered charity.
Registered Company no: 1165130
Registered Charity no: 267523

Paines Plough Offices, Stockroom, 38 Mayton Street, London, N7 6QR

office@painesplough.com
www.painesplough.com

Follow **@PainesPlough** on Twitter
Follow **@painesplough** on Instagram
Like Paines Plough at **facebook.com/PainesPloughHQ**
Donate to Paines Plough at **justgiving.com/PainesPlough**

the
women's
prize
for playwriting

Founded by Ellie Keel and Paines Plough in 2019, the Women's Prize for Playwriting is one step in the movement towards redressing the gender balance of plays produced in our theatres. By seeking out, championing and staging extraordinary new plays by women, we hope to redefine and revitalise the canon for future generations. We work with a judging panel of exceptional leaders in their field to award a cash prize of £12,000 to the winning playwright and produce their play on a major stage in the UK or Ireland. Find out more: www.womensprizeforplaywriting.co.uk

THE TEAM

Founder Director | Ellie Keel

Ellie studied Modern Languages at Oxford University and developed a successful career as a theatre producer before founding the Women's Prize for Playwriting in 2019. She launched the prize with Founding Partner, Paines Plough, after a litany of unacceptable statistics made it clear that plays by women writers were severely underrepresented on national stages in the UK and Ireland.

As Founder Director, Ellie leads on all aspects of strategy, communications and fundraising for the Women's Prize for Playwriting, as well as overseeing the day-to-day operations and administration of the Prize. With Paines Plough, Ellie is also responsible for programming and co-producing plays which win the Women's Prize for Playwriting, and for championing the plays which reach the longlist, shortlist and finalist stages.

Alongside the prize, Ellie is an award-winning theatre and audio producer with her company EKP, which specialises in creating fearlessly imaginative new plays by female and non-binary writers. Her credits include the sell-out shows *HOTTER* and *FITTER* by Mary Higgins and Ell Potter (Soho Theatre, Traverse

Theatre and tour); *Reasons You Should(n't) Love Me* by Amy Trigg (Kiln Theatre, Audible and tour); the multi award-winning *Sap* by Rafaella Marcus (Roundabout, Soho Theatre and tour); *Collapsible* by Margaret Perry (Bush Theatre, HighTide Festival, Abbey Theatre and tour); and *Redefining Juliet* (Barbican Centre).

Ellie is also a writer represented by Cathryn Summerhayes at Curtis Brown. Her first novel, *THE FOUR*, will be published by HarperCollins in April 2024.

Literary Associate | Tommo Fowler
Tommo is a Sheffield-based freelance dramaturg for text and production, and a director.

As Literary Associate of the Women's Prize for Playwriting, he coordinates the submission and reading processes for the Prize, as well as supporting its strategic development.

He is also co-founder of award-winning dramaturgy company RoughHewn (Olwen Wymark Award, Writers' Guild of Great Britain), a Board Member of the Dramaturgs' Network, and a reader for BBC Writers room and the Royal Court. He was previously Residencies Dramaturg and a Supported Artist at Sheffield Theatres, and has been a reader for several other theatres and awards.

As a dramaturg, theatre includes *Jews. In Their Own Words.* (Royal Court); *One Jewish Boy* (Trafalgar Studios); *Out of the Dark* (Rose Theatre, Kingston) and *In My Lungs the Ocean Swells* (VAULT Festival, Origins Award).

JUDGING PANEL 2023
Samira Ahmed, April de Angelis, Chris Bush, Noma Dumezweni, Mel Kenyon, Indhu Rubasingham (Chair), Anya Ryan, Nina Steiger, Katharine Viner.

We are exceptionally grateful to our Advisory Council for their support and expertise: Rosie Allison, Kate Ashton, Kathleen Bacon (Chair), Rupert Gavin, Daisy Goodwin, Raxita Kapashi, Isabel Marr, Tessa Murray.

45North champions, develops, and produces outstanding work by female and non-binary artists. Founded in 2019 and led by the very best creative teams from a variety of performing and producing backgrounds, we continue to reinvest in emerging artists who are beginning and expanding their practices through our seed commission schemes.

45North commits to maintaining creative teams of no less than 75% female or non-binary artists, working to bring inclusive and exciting new theatre and events to London, Edinburgh, across the UK and internationally. Based in Hackney, beginning in 2021, 45North commits to no less than 40% People of the Global Majority across our creative teams.

We take risks to challenge our ideas of self and the world in which we live. We encourage our audiences to do the same.

45North Limited is a private company limited by shares.
Registered Company no: 12259182

45North, Studio 44, Hackney Downs Studios, London E8 2BT
+ 44 (0) 77 0924 6253
admin@forty-fivenorth.com
www.forty-fivenorth.com

Follow @forty_fivenorth on Twitter
Follow @forty_fivenorth on Instagram
Like 45North at facebook.com/45NorthProds
Donate to 45North at www.forty-fivenorth.com/support

THEATRE MADE IN EDINBURGH

ARTISTIC DIRECTOR **DAVID GREIG**
EXECUTIVE DIRECTOR **MIKE GRIFFITHS**

The Royal Lyceum Theatre Edinburgh is the leading producing theatre in Scotland and one of the United Kingdom's most prolific theatre companies.

Our beautiful, intimate Victorian theatre was built in 1883 and has played a significant role in the cultural and creative life of the city and surrounding area for over 140 years. Since 1965, the current Lyceum company has developed a reputation for innovative, high-quality theatre, drawing upon the considerable talent in Scotland as well as developing award winning work with partners across the globe to make theatre in Edinburgh that can speak to the world.

We believe that making and watching theatre together is life enhancing. We are committed to being a theatre rooted in our community, a truly civic theatre entertaining, challenging and inspiring all the people of Edinburgh. To reach the widest possible audience we find new ways to open our doors and stage to the public, as well as reaching out into Edinburgh's schools and neighbourhoods with a range of programmes taking place beyond our walls.

Under Artistic Director David Greig, The Lyceum has continued to seek out new artistic partnerships, casting hundreds of local citizens in our main stage productions. We have made work with Malthouse Theatre, Melbourne; DOT Theatre, Istanbul; Bristol Old Vic; National Theatre of Scotland; Citizens Theatre; Scottish Dance Theatre; Stellar Quines; The Old Vic, Lung Ha Theatre Company and Fueli

For the latest information about The Lyceum visit **lyceum.org.uk**

ALBA | CHRUTHACHAIL

THE CITY OF EDINBURGH COUNCIL

LYCEUM STAFF

Abbie Nicolson Front of House Assistant
Adam Brook Stage Door/Fire Security
Alex Shanks Front of House Assistant
Amie Gilbertson Front of House Assistant
Amy McVicar Front of House Assistant
Andrew Devenport Lighting and Sound Technician
Anna Brooke Front of House Assistant
Annemarie Devlin Director of Development
Anthony Christie Front of House Assistant
Archie Beattie Front of House Assistant
Argyro Sapsouzidi Costume Maker
Avril Gardiner Dresser
Ben Jeffries Director of Communications and Customer Services
Caitlin Higgins Box Office Assistant
Caitlin Mitchard Box Office Assistant
Caitlin Wiedenhof Head of Costume
Cameron Banks Duty Manager
Carol Johnston Executive PA
Chantal Short Dresser
Chelsea Bunyan Front of House Assistant
Chris Townsend Front of House Assistant
Christine Dove Deputy Head of Costume
Claire Loughran Stage Door Receptionist
Claire Williamson Deputy Stage Manager
Clare Rodgers Front of House Assistant
Connel Burnett Creative Learning Assistant Producer
Connor Buchanan Finance Officer
Cris Peploe Front of House Assistant
Dan Dixon Company Stage Manager
Daniel Holden Front of House Assistant
David Butterworth Production Manager
David Dey Producer
David Greig Artistic Director
Debi Pirie Front of House Assistant
Electra McPhillips Development Manager
Emma Hindle Front of House Assistant
Euan McLaren Technical Manager
Fiona Harvey-Jones Director of Estates and Facilities
Gavin Dunbar Box Office Deputy Manager

Gavin Roberts Maintenance Cleaner
Georgia Traquair-Stewart Front of House Assistant
Gillian Brook Stage Door Receptionist
Grazyna Wysocka Costume Maker
Gregor Weir Production Assistant
Hamish Millar Head of Stage
Hannah Bradley Front of House Assistant
Hannah Edie Theatre in Residence Drama Artist
Hannah Roberts Producer
Harry Carrington Marketing Officer
Heather Johns Creative Learning Officer
Heather Maxwell Front of House Assistant
Helen Steel Front of House Assistant
Ian Cunningham Lighting and Sound Technician
Ian Gibson Head of Lighting and Sound
Isidora Bouziouri Front of House Assistant
Jack Oliver Front of House Assistant
Jack Summers-McKay Events Manager
Jackie Crichton Literary Associate
Jaime Foster Director of Finance and Administration
Jaïrus Obayomi Front of House Assistant
James Kinnear Front of House Assistant
Jane Black Front of House Assistant
Jessica Moran FOH Services Manager
Joana Inacio Front of House Assistant
Joe Eaton Front of House Assistant
John Heron Stage Technician/Flyman
Jules Fraser Duty Manager
Justin Connolly Box Office Manager
Karen Sorley Costume Cutter
Kate Leiper Stage Door/Fire Security
Katie Fraser Duty Manager
Katie Sumi Development and Database Administrator
Katy Bancroft Creative Learning Intern
Kerrie Walker Creative Learning Producer
Kevin Duff Stage Technician
Kikelomo Hassan Front of House Assistant
Laura Gentile Front of House Assistant
Laura Kwiatkowski Front of House Assistant
Leila Price Creative Learning Assistant

Lesley Gardner Front of House Assistant
Lindsey Bell Deputy Head of Lighting and Sound
Liz King Director of Producing
Liz Marsh Lighting Engineer
Liz Moon Marketing and Communications Manager
Louise Sertoglu HR Manager
Lucy Deere Producer
Malcolm McQuillan Maintenance Cleaner
Maria Chirca Deputy Head of Lighting and Sound
Maria Papageorgiou Front of House Assistant
Mike Griffiths Executive Director
Molly Gilroy Marketing Officer
Morgan Yates Senior Stage Technician
Morris Jeffries Front of House Assistant
Olivia McGeachy Front of House Assistant
Rebecca Wicksted Front of House Assistant
Robbie Castle Front of House Assistant
Robin Crane Senior Stage Technician
Ross McFarlane Deputy Head of Lighting and Sound
Ross Sibbald Maintenance Cleaner
Rowan Berry Front of House Assistant
Rowan Milne Front of House Assistant
Russell Gray Maintenance Cleaner
Russell Kemp Box Office Supervisor
Sam Trotter Front of House Assistant
Sandy Bishop Front of House Assistant
Sarah Gallagher Front of House Assistant
Sarah Greger Finance Manager
Sharon May Director of Creative Learning
Sofia Garcia Ruiz Front of House Assistant
Sophie Howell Creative Learning Officer
Susan Craig Front of House Assistant
Tim Primrose Stage Door/Fire Security
Tony Everitt Buildings Maintenance and Services Manager
Vix Garner FOH Operations Manager
Wendy McEwan Front of House Assistant
Zoe King Assistant Stage Manager
Zuzanna Grajzer Box Office Assistant

ORANGE TREE THEATRE

A powerhouse of independent theatre

The Orange Tree (OT) is an award-winning, independent theatre. Recognised as a powerhouse that creates high-quality productions of new and rediscovered plays, we entertain 70,000 people across the UK every year.

The OT's home in Richmond, South West London, is an intimate theatre with the audience seated all around the stage: watching a performance here is truly a unique experience.

We believe in the power of dramatic stories to entertain, thrill and challenge us; plays that enrich our lives by enhancing our understanding of ourselves and each other.

As a registered charity (266128) sitting at the heart of its community, we work with 10,000 people in Richmond and beyond through participatory theatre projects for everyone.

The Orange Tree Theatre's mission is to enable audiences to experience the next generation of theatre talent, experiment with ground-breaking new drama and explore the plays from the past that inspire the theatre-makers of the present. To find out how you can help us to do that you can visit **orangetreetheatre.co.uk/discover**

orangetreetheatre.co.uk

Registered charity no. 266128

Front of House Manager **Paul Bradley**
Technical Director **Stuart Burgess**
Marketing Officer **Anna Charlesworth**
Finance Manager **Caroline Goodwin**
Technical Manager **Lisa Hood**
Development & Communications Director **Alex Jones**
Literary Associate **Guy Jones**

Artistic Director **Tom Littler**
Admin & Sales Assistant **Hannah McLelland**
General Manager **Sarah Murray**
Company Stage Manager **Jenny Skivens**
Development Officer **Jess Straub**
Executive Director **Hanna Streeter**
Community Manager **Stella Taljaard**
Marketing Manager **Rachel Wood**
Resident Assistant Director **Sam Woof**

BRISTOL OLD VIC

Built in 1766 as a place where the people of Bristol could come together, Bristol Old Vic is the oldest continuously working theatre in the English-speaking world.

Our mission is to create pioneering twenty-first-century theatre in partnership with the people of our energetic city; inspired by the history and magical design of the most beautiful playhouse in the country.

We aim to inspire audiences with our own original productions, both at home and on tour, whilst nurturing the next generation of artists, whether that be through our 350-strong Young Company, our many outreach and education projects or our trailblazing artist development programme, Bristol Ferment.

We are publicly funded by Arts Council England and Bristol City Council, using that investment to support experiment and innovation, to allow access to our programme for people who would not otherwise encounter it or be able to afford it and to keep our extraordinary heritage alive and animated.

In 2018, we completed our two-year multi-million-pound redevelopment project, which transformed our front of house space into a warm and welcoming public building for all of Bristol to enjoy, created a new studio theatre and opened up our unique theatrical heritage to the public for the first time.

Since 2020, we have been sharing our shows in new ways: Live Broadcast from our Georgian auditorium to tens of thousands and made available On Demand; sharing live interactive theatre events and Q&As; and bringing some of our biggest shows to TV. This has led to the launch of Bristol Old Vic On Screen – unforgettable performances filmed in our 256-year-old theatre, broadcast live to you wherever you are in the world.

What's On / Book Tickets:
0117 987 7877 | bristololdvic.org.uk

Sign up / follow us for the latest:

Supported using public funding by
ARTS COUNCIL ENGLAND
Charity No. 228235

A NOTE FROM ELLIE KEEL, FOUNDER OF THE WOMEN'S PRIZE FOR PLAYWRITING

I vividly remember the first time I read *You Bury Me*. I was walking across Westminster Bridge on a summer evening in 2020, and one of our Women's Prize reading team sent me an email flagging it as one of the best scripts they'd read. Their message was so enthusiastic that I opened the play and read the first page – and then the second, the third and the fourth. Then I hopped on a bus so I could sit down and read some more.

The play sucked me into a very different city. It drew me into dusty, crowded, sweltering Cairo, where the lives and loves of six young people were playing out amidst enormous tension and oppression. It was full of high hopes and impossible dreams; youthful anguish and bitter frustration; prejudice and conflict and passionate love. Its dialogue was funny and playful and tender. It was very readable but I found myself immediately visualising it on stage – always a good sign.

When the judges met in October 2020 their acclaim for *You Bury Me* was unanimous. They applauded the play's universality – the characters seem to transcend their very specific setting and communicate the heightened emotions of young people everywhere. They also admired Ahlam's rhythmically beautiful writing and captivating imagery, and the delicacy and ease with which she conjures setting and character. For most audiences, Cairo is a new world but Ahlam takes us there effortlessly, immersing us in the vivid, painful lives of these characters and this city.

This is the kind of unique, fearless and hugely entertaining play I dreamed of finding when I founded the Women's Prize for Playwriting. I hope you enjoy experiencing it for the first time as much as I did.

Ellie Keel
Founder Director, the Women's Prize for Playwriting

DIRECTOR'S NOTE

I can't talk about this play without talking about its beating heart. It is the cradle that holds the character, the story, 'The City'.

From the first conversations with Ahlam, I could feel this deep, painful, conflicted love pour out of her when she spoke of Cairo. She shared stories about the world she grew up in, the laughter, the pain, the politics, and that feeling of loss and searing grief over what it means to love her city. Over these endless chats and coffees, I understood how deeply she felt for all of the characters in her play. It drew me in, made me want to explore more, and attempt to understand the many layers to Egypt.

This play was made with love by so many wonderful people who have spoken with truth, joy and wisdom, and we see the story through their eyes. It has been joyful, inspiring and beautiful. It belongs to the memories of the people, the land and the soil that holds them. I feel forever changed by them.

This city, this play, has lived with me, and lingers forever inside of me. Forever moved, enlivened, angry, galvanised and ready, ready never ever to forget.

I hope the play will do the same to you.

Katie

WRITER'S NOTE

This play is about many things, it's about youth, it's about revolution, it's about violence, it's about love. Beyond that, this play is a love letter to Cairo, a love letter to the people of Cairo. Particularly to the people of Cairo who stood in Tahrir Square in 2011, demanding a better world for themselves and for others. This play can only capture a fragment of that world that I grew up in, and a sliver of the city that raised me. But what I hope that this play does is honour my peers, many of whom are present in these characters I've written. These are people I grew up with, people I went to school with, people I cried to in the middle of the night and laughed with till the early morning, people who would drive an extra hour out of their way just to make sure I'd get home safe, these are people I joyfully debated and argued with over beer and termes, people I danced and flirted with, people I've built dreams with, people I've heard about through gossip, people who have inspired me, people I've shared rides with, people I've been stuck in traffic with for hours with, people I've watched overthrow a government, people I've watched organise campaign after campaign for human rights and personal safety, people I've supported through loss and heartbreak (both personal and political), people who supported me through the alienation that is specific to migration while still clashing with riot police regularly, people who helped me fall in love with a city I grew up resenting, these are people I fell in love with, people I fell out with and made up with, people I admired from afar, people who are still processing the trauma of what happened in 2011, and the trauma of what has happened since, people who are not allowed to mourn their dead, people who are not allowed to celebrate their memories. This play is dedicated most of all to those who have lost their lives to the Mubarak regime and every government that followed. To those who lost their lives to incarceration and exile, to those who have had their lives taken from them and to those who made the excruciating decision to take their own. This play was written as an act of mourning, as an act of honouring, and most of all, as an act of love. I hope this play offers that space to all: to those of us who were in Tahrir Square, and those of us who were not.

CHARACTERS

ALIA – An Egyptian. 22 years old. She has just graduated with an Engineering degree from Cairo University. She comes from a conservative Muslim family. Her paternal lineage have all served or are serving in the police. She's in love with Tamer.

TAMER – An Egyptian. 22 years old. He has also graduated with an Engineering degree from Cairo University. He comes from a traditional Christian family. Christians in Egypt are primarily Copts (Egyptian Orthodox Christians). He's in love with Alia.

LINA – An Egyptian. 17 years old. She's in high school. She comes from a traditional Christian family. She's still in the process of discovering her sexuality and gender.

MAYA – An Egyptian. 18 years old. She's in the same high school as Lina. She comes from a left-leaning family, so her family aren't religious. They might be more agnostic or atheist but they don't label themselves as such, you could say they're culturally Muslim. Her parents are divorced and Osman is her half brother (same father).

OSMAN – An Egyptian. 25 years old. He's a journalist and blogger. He was very active during the Egyptian uprising and wrote extensively about it. He's in love with Zeina, a staunch political activist.

RAFIK – An Egyptian. 25 years old. He graduated with a degree in English literature from Cairo University. After graduating, he didn't know what he wanted to do and decided to just smoke his problems away.

THE CITY – The city narrates, explains, confuses, comforts, challenges, shares its stories. The city should be played by all of the actors in the play.

SETTING

Cairo

TIME

This play starts in 2015.

AUTHOR'S NOTES

تقبرني (to'-bor-ni): Lit. 'You bury me'. A saying in Levantine Arabic used to express affection and love. 'May you bury me' is a declaration that one does not want to live without a loved one (or loved thing).

This play is dedicated to Cairo, and to all those who (are cursed enough to) love her.

PROLOGUE: WELCOME TO CAIRO

(**THE CITY** *enters.*)

THE CITY. In 2011, Egypt had a revolution.

We have to mention this because it's been a long time.

And you might not know.

Or maybe you forgot.

That's what's scary.

That we will all forget.

We had demonstrations all across Egypt.

But all eyes were on Cairo.

The beating heart of the country.

Cairo isn't the beating heart.

More like the liver.

The swollen, sick, failing liver.

It can be both.

It's the beating heart and the failing liver.

A government

No.

A Dictator.

No.

A Tyrant

Good one.

A tyrant dictator and his government... was overthrown.

A regime collapsed and –

A new era began.

What we want you to understand is the revolution politicised a generation.

My generation.

Our generation.

Our degenerate, whiny, good-for-nothing, spoilt, shitty, millennial generation.

What we want you to understand is that in 2011 we were on the brink of creating a different world for ourselves.

One in which we weren't helpless, useless, powerless in the gnarled claws of decaying regimes.

One in which we weren't running to the West only to be called terrorists, barbarians, and thrown back into the sea.

We were pushing back. We pushed and pushed, and for just a moment, we tasted freedom.

Not quite.

We tasted freedom.

We were able to imagine the *possibility* of tasting freedom.

I actually *tasted* freedom.

Would you both just shut up?

This story isn't even about 2011.

This story isn't about that... dream.

This is a story about death.

The death of that dream.

This is about 2015.

About that feeling.

That feeling of the beginning of the end.

You know that feeling?

I mean, we all know that feeling these days.

As we plummet to our doom.

You know that existential horror?

Of just watching it all go completely to fuck?

In Egypt we know that feeling well.

For our generation, 2015 is when we experienced the dying embers of hope.

This is when our story set.

As for the where...

Cairo.

The thing about Cairo is...

The thing that sets Cairo apart is that...

It's that –

Apart from what?

What's it apart from?

Yeah, why are we being vague?

Why does Cairo always have to be special?

It always thinks it's so fucking special

Full of attention-seeking little –

This could be anywhere

But it's not

It's this city

Our city.

The city is us!

We are the city!

Stop fucking around.

We're talking about –

Cairo. We're talking about Cairo.

We are –

THE THING ABOUT CAIRO IS

OSMAN. She's all layers.

> (**THE CITY** *explodes to life. It's Mercedes Benz
> and donkey carts. It's exhaust fumes, shisha
> smoke, grit, and grime. It's pedestrians
> snaking through rows of cars. It's hustlers and
> beggars and people trying to get by. It's veg
> and fruit vendors, 'roba bikya' carts and kids
> selling lemons. It's men selling grilled corn
> and roasted sweet potatoes. It's football games
> through small radios and old televisions.
> It's policemen discreetly snoring at embassy
> doors. It's celebrations on colourful boats on
> the Nile. It's the echoes of calls to prayer from
> higher ground. It's lively conversations over
> iced frappes. It's lively conversations over
> liver sandwiches. It's a family of six riding
> a motorbike at high speed on the bridge. It's
> the slow traffic beeping its way through the
> sunset, towards The City of the Dead.)*

Scene One

THE CITY. In this city...

We stay up late.

We also wake up late.

We're also late to everything all the time.

It's not personal.

It's cultural!

We are the city that never sleeps.

And here we have Osman.

Osman wants to sleep.

He wants to sleep so badly.

> (**OSMAN** *is pacing at his desk. His laptop is open. He is trying to find the right words.*)

OSMAN. The thing about Cairo is... it's all layers.

It's all Mercedes and donkey carts. It's exhaust fumes and smoke and grit... No.

This city...

> (*He sits down at his laptop. He writes.*)

This city cannot be defined. Not in the traditional sense. It is not a homogenous space. It is not a coherent space. To be Cairo one must accept the contradictions, the paradox of life, making existence an oxymoron. We are not a singular way of life, not a singular way of thinking, we are not a singular culture, as aggressive as the national project tries to be. We need to think of a different way of being and thus of governing. The revolution and its failure made this clear. We need to organise with those we disagree with, the moment we compete for power it all falls apart. Power is in the collective, the revolution proved this as well.

My question is how can we learn from this city? How can we learn to hold multitudes within ourselves? How do we find harmony in opposition? How can we hold on to love when we are surrounded by death?

We may not be able to resist in our streets, but let's keep asking questions, let's keep learning from this ancient city because I'm not ready to give into despair.

We can do better than another military regime. We deserve better.

The revolution lives on comrades. In our hearts and in our minds.

(He uploads the blog post.)

Scene Two

THE CITY. Meet Tamer.

Tamer's idea of love came from films.

American rom coms.

Egyptian black and white films.

And the occasional fluffy French film.

Stories full of boy meets girl.

Boy falls for girl.

Girl either immediately or eventually falls for boy.

He always wondered if he was leading man material.

Was he more Omar Sharif or Keanu Reeves?

Was he more George Clooney or Rushdy Abaza?

He always believed that there would only be One. One who will capture his imagination and grip his...

Heart?

Thoughts?

Soul?

SOUL!

Tamer believed in soulmates.

Every girl that crossed his path was potentially The One.

He didn't fall in love with every girl he met.

But well...

He considered it.

Because he's a sap.

No, don't say that. He's romantic.

He's cringe.

He's not.

Enough!

Tamer believed in soulmates.

Because maybe just maybe...

That look...

That closeness...

That accidental hand brush...

> (**TAMER** *and* **ALIA** *are sitting on the corniche, looking at all the lights dancing, reflecting in the Nile, music plays in the distance. They are both in their early twenties.)*

TAMER. So...?

ALIA. So?

TAMER. What am I doing here?

ALIA. I ... I don't know.

TAMER. Right.

ALIA. I miss you.

TAMER. ...

I'm sorry but... I can't.

ALIA. No wait.

You don't want me anymore?

TAMER. Alia... No. That's not fair. You know how I feel! I think I've made it absolutely clear what I want. You're the one that ended it, you're the one that said –

ALIA. I want you.

TAMER. ...

ALIA. I can't help it.

TAMER. No... I ... Not again – You, you, you said that –

ALIA. I love you.

TAMER. ...

ALIA. There. I said it.

TAMER. ...

ALIA. ...please say something.

TAMER. We can't keep doing this. I don't know how to... deal with this.

ALIA. Do you want to stop speaking to me?

TAMER. No. No, of course not.

ALIA. ...

TAMER. What is wrong with us?

ALIA. I don't know.

> (**TAMER** *holds her hand.* **ALIA** *is trying not to show how ecstatic she is.*)

I ... Tamer, I want to kiss you.

TAMER. Really?

ALIA. Yes. I really want to.

> (**TAMER** *looks around to make sure no one is looking.*)
>
> (*He looks at* **ALIA**, *takes a deep breath and... finally they kiss and its joyous.*)
>
> (**ALIA** *and* **TAMER** *break away. They make sure no one is watching. They steal another quick, blissful kiss.*)

Scene Three

THE CITY. You see, Osman is what some people call…a writer?

A revolutionary!

A woke flake socialist bro man.

No.

Too much?

Just no.

Osman started out as a blogger.

Yes!

The golden age of blogging.

When blogs were deep.

And personal.

Insightful.

Thoughtful.

Witty.

Fun.

He blogged and posted.

He organised and strategized.

He debated and learned.

And he met Zeina.

Zeina.

Now Zeina really is revolutionary.

Some people say she's too much.

Some people say she's too provocative.

Some people say she's too angry.

And why shouldn't she be?

There's lots to be angry about.

Zeina does not take shit from anyone.

Including Osman.

And he loves that about her.

And these days he has trouble sleeping.

When he's not with her.

> *(Suddenly there's knocking on a door. It's a Dokki flat, a phone is ringing.* **OSMAN** *appears. His phone has woken him up. The knocking has disoriented him.)*

OSMAN. Shit.

Hello?

RAFIK. Osman!

OSMAN. Rafik? Are you there?

RAFIK. Yes! I'm outside –

OSMAN. Call the police. I mean, I think the police is at my door. Call Zeina!

RAFIK. It's not the police, it's –

OSMAN. What? Who else would it be? Who would knock at this hour?

RAFIK. Do you really think the police fucking knock?

OSMAN. Of course the police knock first... they're thugs but they don't just smash people's doors in.

RAFIK. Osman listen to me –

OSMAN. I don't know what you're saying.

RAFIK. I'm outside!

OSMAN. Outside of what?

RAFIK. The door. I'm standing in front of the door.

OSMAN. What door?

RAFIK. YOUR door. The knocking is me you idiot!

OSMAN. You're knocking?

RAFIK. Fuck's sake. OPEN THE FUCKING DOOR.

>   (**OSMAN** *opens the door,* **RAFIK** *is standing there with a big bag.*)

OSMAN. What are you doing here? What time is it?

>   (*Call to prayer starts.*)

RAFIK. It's four!

OSMAN. What is going on?

RAFIK. I need a place to crash. Can I stay here for a bit?

OSMAN. Yeah sure, of course.

RAFIK. My dad kicked me out.

OSMAN. Again?

RAFIK. Yes.

OSMAN. Hash?

RAFIK. No.

OSMAN. Sex?

RAFIK. He finally told me that I was adopted and wouldn't be able to inherit his fortune anyway, so I was like 'I'm done with this, I'm out' –

OSMAN. Porn?

RAFIK. Who gets kicked out because of porn?

OSMAN. So what is it?

RAFIK. Told him I'm an atheist.

OSMAN. But you're not.

RAFIK. We had a fight, he threatened me with a knife, my mother cried, my sister had to step in to protect me. You know, the usual.

OSMAN. Right, I don't need to know.

RAFIK. He caught me with a boy.

OSMAN. Caught you? You brought a boy to the house?

RAFIK. Where else were we going to go?

OSMAN. You're awful at this.

RAFIK. At what?

OSMAN. Dating men obviously.

RAFIK. First of all, you don't get to say that because you know nothing about it. And second, you are a shit friend.

OSMAN. You're banging on my door at four a.m.

RAFIK. You know that dating men is uncharted territory for me, and you shouldn't –

OSMAN. Alright. I'm sorry.

Are you okay?

RAFIK. I'm homeless, but otherwise all good.

OSMAN. Obviously make yourself at home. Stay as long as you need.

Spliff?

RAFIK. No, I'm good.

OSMAN. ...?

RAFIK. When would I ever say no?

(The call to prayer continues. **OSMAN** *and* **RAFIK** *listen. They smoke.)*

Would you rather be attractive and boring or unattractive and interesting?

OSMAN. Unattractive and interesting.

RAFIK. Really?

OSMAN. No one wants to be around boring people.

RAFIK. Everyone wants to be around attractive people. That's what attractive means.

OSMAN. Boring people though...

(*They smoke.*)

I'm going back to sleep. You know where the sheets are?

RAFIK. Yeah don't worry about me man.

OSMAN. Great. You know the rules, no blasting Mounir at seven in the morning. No singing Adele at the top of your lungs. And absolutely no MTM played in this house. Ever.

RAFIK. You are so... boring.

OSMAN. I'm serious.

RAFIK. OK... what about Shakira?

OSMAN. Rafik.

RAFIK. I'll be on best behaviour. Promise.

OMAR. Goodnight.

RAFIK. May you wake up to a better world.

OSMAN. Don't make me regret letting you stay.

(**RAFIK** *continues to smoke.*)

Scene Four

*(Detention at a high school. **LINA** is writing
her one hundred lines, **MAYA** is bored and not
writing. They are both in their last year of
high school.)*

THE CITY. The first time a boy tried to kiss Maya was in
the fourth grade.

He went up to her.

Puckered his lips.

And she wacked him right in the eye.

He called her a

'Dumb bitch!'

And ran off.

That was the first time anyone had ever called her a

'Dumb bitch!'

But it wouldn't be the last.

Within minutes Maya is being sent to the principal's
office.

They tell her off.

They say respectable girls don't behave this way.

They say it's her fault because she spends too much
time playing with boys.

They call her mother.

Her mother is furious.

Livid.

Completely and utterly enraged.

Not with Maya.

With the school.

She demands the boy is punished.

The entire ride home, she swears and calls her teachers idiots.

At home, her mother sits her down and tells her she did the right thing.

And then she says

"If that little shit tries it again, kick him in the balls."

MAYA. Did you ever think about having a makeover?

LINA. Sorry?

MAYA. A makeover. You know, like in *She's All That*.

LINA. She's All That?

MAYA. Yeah, that old movie. Have you seen it?

LINA. I think so. Doesn't she just get a haircut? Not exactly a makeover.

MAYA. Haircut can make all the difference, have you seen Ms. Shereen?

LINA. Yeah but –

MAYA. A new haircut and a new outfit, and you'll be smoking hot.

LINA. I don't really care about all that.

MAYA. Well, that's a shame. Have you seen your eyes?

LINA. Thanks?

MAYA. I can make you look incredible. Let's do it. It'll be fun.

LINA. Why are you talking to me?

MAYA. I've always wanted to do the makeover thing, but I've never met someone who needed it.

We can have drinks at mine afterwards, do you drink?

LINA. A little...

MAYA. I knew there was something about you. The quiet ones are always a little wild.

LINA. I don't know if I would call myself wild...

MAYA. It's a compliment, wild is fun.

Thursday good for you? Makeover and drinks?

LINA. I don't... I –

MAYA. Come on!

LINA. Okay, yes.

Thursday's fine.

Scene Five

THE CITY. This city has a way of...

Shoving God down your throat.

I wasn't going to say that but...

It's accurate.

Come on, that's a bit over the top.

It's exactly like that.

And God stays stuck there.

It's not like that.

It is a bit.

God stays stuck there, nowhere to go, nowhere to grow.

We're a spiritual people!

No, we're not.

Not all spiritual.

We're so fucking spiritual.

It's just that sometimes... we forget.

The God in our throats isn't ours.

That's the problem.

Like when Rafik first started doubting his belief in God.

He was twelve.

He felt he couldn't tell a soul.

And then in high school he was told to keep his doubts to himself.

He started to interpret God as love.

God is love and God loves you no matter what.

For him that made love divine and for a while, that was enough.

He felt he could breathe a bit.

Then in university.

He met a woman.

A woman that would change everything.

She believed nothing.

She said things he didn't allow himself to think.

She terrified him.

And he could not stop thinking about her.

He lost God.

And fell into her.

He lost himself.

The ground he walked on fell away and then –

She left him.

No, he left her.

I'm pretty sure she left him.

It doesn't matter!

The point is he was in free fall.

Then the revolution happened.

And he felt the God in his throat dislodge and spread.

Spread all over.

Spread through him.

He finally understood what it meant for a body to be sacred.

For *his* body to be sacred.

See? That's what I meant.

We're a spiritual people.

> (**RAFIK** *is sitting on the couch, spaced out, he grabs a book and begins to read.*)
>
> (*He struggles to focus. He throws the book back on the table.*)

RAFIK. Fuck it.

> (**OSMAN** *bursts in. He quickly strips as much off his clothes as is appropriately possible. He stands in front of the fan or air conditioning.*)

The electricity's cut.

OSMAN.   Fuck this dicksucking, cuntfingering, motherfucking piece of shit cock of a day!

RAFIK. Rough day?

OSMAN. Cairo I fucking hate you, you soul-sucking, spirit-crushing bitch of a city!

RAFIK. You done?

OSMAN. SHIT. FUCK. BALLS.

RAFIK. ...

OSMAN. OK I'm done.

> (**OSMAN** *sits on the couch. On cue,* **RAFIK** *begins to roll a joint.*)

Thank fuck you didn't finish it all today. I seriously would have thrown you out the window.

RAFIK. Which window would you choose? Your bedroom window into the back alley? Or the living room window into the main street?

OSMAN. What difference does it make?

RAFIK. What effect are you going for, shock or mystery?

OSMAN. Shock. Always shock.

RAFIK. Living room window.

*(They start smoking. **OSMAN** visibly relaxes.)*

Your mom stopped by this afternoon.

OSMAN. Yeah?

RAFIK. Brought you some food. Said something about you being too skinny.

OSMAN. Did you eat it all?

RAFIK. What kind of friend do you think I am? I left you some.

OSMAN. How was your day?

RAFIK. The usual. I've been trying to read for the past two hours, keep reading the same sentence over and over again, it's a nightmare.

OSMAN. Maybe you should try getting a job.

RAFIK. And become a good boy like you?

OSMAN. Do you know how long you're gonna be staying?

RAFIK. Look, if it's a problem for me –

OSMAN. No, no problem.

What I mean is, have you talked to your family at all?

RAFIK. No, you know what they're like.

OSMAN. Do you have a plan?

RAFIK. Of course.

OSMAN. Yeah?

RAFIK. I'm gonna seduce a rich western woman and –

OSMAN. Rafik I'm serious.

RAFIK. OK. The plan is to go to Sinai and sell all the drugs to hippy Israelis.

OSMAN. Rafik...

RAFIK. OK, OK, for real. I've thought about it, and I think it's time for me to pursue my dream of becoming Egypt's first Coptic Christian coach of the national football team.

OSMAN. Has there never been a Christian coach of the national team?

RAFIK. Fuck knows. I hate football.

(*They smoke.*)

OSMAN. They're monitoring Grindr by the way.

RAFIK. Who's they?

OSMAN. The pope. Who do you think? They're using Grindr to arrest people.

So... you know, you should probably delete the app.

RAFIK. Do I look like someone that uses Grindr? Come on man, I'm classier than that.

OSMAN. Rafik. Delete it. Now.

RAFIK. OK ...what about I delete the app and you take a break from writing on your blog?

OSMAN. Don't be ridiculous.

RAFIK. Look, I know you're worried about me. But I'm also worried about you.

OSMAN. Don't be.

RAFIK. Well, I am. This is one of the most dangerous countries to be a journalist just now. Or have you not heard the news?

OSMAN. They would have taken me already if they wanted to.

RAFIK. You don't know that. You don't know how this security apparatus thinks.

OSMAN. I do know that using Grindr is more high risk just now.

RAFIK. It's incredible that you're sitting here right now. Alive and well.

OSMAN. I'm not going to let them intimidate me.

RAFIK. Why do you have to be such an unbearable martyr?

OSMAN. Why do you have to be such a passive prick?

RAFIK. Take a break and I will delete the app.

OSMAN. ...

I'll think about it.

I'm going to head off. I'm not coming home tonight, staying over at Zeina's.

RAFIK. What? But I thought tonight was movie night.

OSMAN. I ...we can watch a movie some other time.

RAFIK. No, no we can't. We said movie night tonight. I bought the movie hash already.

OSMAN. There's no such thing as movie hash.

RAFIK. There is. It's the hash I bought specifically for movie night, and if you abandon our tradition tonight then I'm smoking it all on my own.

OSMAN. ...

RAFIK. I've also got a superb selection tonight. For the classic category we've got Hadutta Masreya,

OSMAN. ...

RAFIK. For cinematic art we've got The Science of Sleep –

OSMAN. No...

RAFIK. And for the cringe category we have the film that ruled the world, *Titanic*.

OSMAN. Seriously?

RAFIK. You are such a snob.

OSMAN. I'm not going to say to Zeina that I'm not coming over because I need to watch *Titanic*.

RAFIK. If you gave Zeina the choice then I'm sure she'd choose *Titantic*.

OSMAN. Well we could ask her and invite her over?

RAFIK. No! This is our thing! We can do group movie night some other time.

OSMAN. ...

Fine. Fuck it.

RAFIK. Yes!

OSMAN. No *Titanic* though.

RAFIK. We'll see.

OSMAN. I mean it.

RAFIK. Sure.

OSMAN. Rafik.

(**RAFIK** *looks at* **OSMAN** *mischievously.*)

Don't.

(**RAFIK** *blasts a song in the style of* [**"MY HEART WILL GO ON"**] *by Celine Dion.*)

Scene Six

THE CITY. In 1997 this city (like the rest of the world) fell in love with the film *Titanic*.

We fell in love with love.

We fell in love with Jack and Rose.

We fell in love with Leo.

He was so pretty.

Of course, this love had no sex.

We didn't see much of THE scene.

The paint me like your French girls scene.

That's what I mean by THE scene.

The point is, there's no sex.

Leo's focused eyes.

And cut.

Kate's focused eyes.

And cut.

Plot points.

And cut.

A handprint on a steamed window.

And cut.

Sanitised love.

Clean love.

Clean minds.

That's the mistake they made.

Clean minds.

No such thing.

With every cut.

Was a world of questions.

And filth.

Ew.

It's the truth!

But for Alia...

Yes Alia. Right.

Her idea of love came from what she knew she didn't want.

She didn't want empty promises.

She didn't want someone that would make her feel small.

She didn't want to get caught up in the romance of it all.

She would not be duped by sentimental artists.

She would not be duped by poetry and drama and desire and –

She would not be duped by *Titanic*!

At least that's what she told herself.

>   (*In a café somewhere like Mohandessin or Nasr City,* **ALIA** *and* **TAMER** *are sitting across from one another.*)

ALIA. I told her that I can't do all the work, she needs to step up, you know?

TAMER. Uh-huh

ALIA. She's done this before, remember Dr. Samir's project?

TAMER. Yeah

ALIA. Tamer are you even listening?

TAMER. Sorry, I was just distracted.

ALIA. Distracted by what?

TAMER. You.

ALIA. Eh?

TAMER. You're really beautiful.

ALIA. Okay, Tamer...

TAMER. I swear, I just... I really want to kiss you right now.

ALIA. Tamer, someone might hear.

TAMER. I really do. I want to kiss you and...

ALIA. And...?

TAMER. I want to do other things as well...

ALIA. Tamer!

TAMER. What? I wanna do good things.

I want to touch you.

ALIA. You can hold my hand.

TAMER. I love holding your hand... but I want to touch you in other places as well.

ALIA. Tamer...

TAMER. I'm not talking about there. I wanna hold you, and sleep next to you, and when you're ready I want to –

ALIA. You need to stop.

TAMER. Sorry.

ALIA. Don't feel bad. It's just... I really want that as well.

TAMER. I want to love all of you.

ALIA. I want that also. I want to be with you.

>   (*Under the table,* **ALIA** *starts to touch* **TAMER**
>   *with her foot, she gets close to his crotch but*
>   *doesn't quite touch it.*)

TAMER. What are you doing?

ALIA. I want to touch you as well.

TAMER. Okay you need to stop.

ALIA. You don't like it?

TAMER. No! No, it's not that. It's the opposite actually.

ALIA. So should I continue or not?

TAMER. Aaah, no, no you need to stop otherwise I won't
be able to get up.

ALIA. Get it up?

TAMER. No, I mean, I won't be able to stand up.

ALIA. That's a good thing right?

TAMER. No. I mean, yes.

ALIA. I thought you liked this?

TAMER. I don't know. I just...

Stop.

ALIA. Why?

TAMER. Really, you need to – please... stop.

ALIA. What if I don't want to?

TAMER. Alia, enough!

ALIA. Okay.

>   (**ALIA** *stops what she's doing. She's annoyed.*)

TAMER. Alia...

ALIA. It's fine. If that's what you want.

TAMER. Alia please don't start.

ALIA. Start what? I was talking about my project, you're the one that started –

TAMER. Okay, yes. I'm sorry, I was just trying to tell you I love you.

ALIA. Were you now? Trying to say I love you. Well next time just try saying it instead of talking about all this touching business.

TAMER. I did say it.

ALIA. Did you start with saying it? No, no you didn't. Because all you think about is sex.

TAMER. Lower your voice.

ALIA. You guys are all the same. That's all you care about.

TAMER. That's not true.

ALIA. And then when I actually give it a go, no that's wrong.

TAMER. I didn't say it was wrong!

ALIA. When you do it, it's romantic and sexy –

TAMER. That's not fair –

ALIA. – but when I do it then it's risky and bad.

TAMER. You're overreacting.

ALIA. I'm overreacting?

TAMER. A little, yes.

ALIA. No, Tamer, I'm leaving.

TAMER. Alia.

ALIA. Don't touch me!

TAMER. Please, wait –

*(**ALIA** leaves. **TAMER** wants to chase her but can't...)*

Alia, come back! Shit.

Scene Seven

THE CITY. Lina changed schools when it came time to go to high school.

Should we tell them about how the education system in Egypt works?

(*They considers this.*)

Nah!

We're not going to slow down the story for that.

Just tell them the very crucial bits.

Basically, Lina's parents decided to switch her to an international school system.

It was quite a bit more expensive, but they thought it would improve her chances of getting a degree abroad.

If she wanted to.

They couldn't afford it for both their children, so they gambled on Lina.

Their brighter one.

They didn't think of how the switch would affect her.

New school.

New rules.

A different culture almost.

People here spoke more English and could barely speak Arabic.

The teachers had no control over students.

She was sure the principal received bribes from parents.

Girls wore tighter clothes and flirted openly with boys.

Boys teased them by pinching their waists.

They touched at every opportunity and every touch would linger.

And even though they were told off by teachers, it wouldn't stop them.

Of course, there were rules here as well.

There were boundaries.

And if those boundaries were crossed then you would be called a slut.

And sometimes you were called a slut anyway.

Lina had a hard time keeping up.

So she mostly kept to herself.

She might become an accidental slut.

And no one wants that.

> (**LINA** *and* **MAYA** *are in* **MAYA**'s *room,* **LINA** *has had her makeover and isn't entirely convinced, they're drinking ID vodkas.*)

LINA. I'm not so sure about this top.

MAYA. What are you talking about? It looks great.

LINA. I guess...

Is your mom here?

MAYA. Don't worry about her. She works late.

LINA. Does she know you drink?

MAYA. Kind of. She said I can drink once I'm in university.

LINA. But we're not in uni.

MAYA. We're basically in uni so it's fine.

LINA. My mother would never let me drink in the house.

MAYA. Are you parents religious?

LINA. Not really. They're just a bit... strict.

MAYA. I don't know what I'd do if my mum was strict.

LINA. Do you live with just your mum?

MAYA. Yup. My parents got divorced when I was a baby. My dad's on wife number four. I've got two half brothers and a stepsister.

Any more questions about my family?

LINA. Sorry. I guess I'm just a bit curious.

MAYA. It's okay, I don't mind.

LINA. Which university are you gonna go to?

MAYA. I want to go abroad.

LINA. Abroad?

MAYA. Somewhere like Europe or the States. Somewhere I can finally breathe.

LINA. If you could choose though, where would you go?

MAYA. Scotland.

LINA. Why?

MAYA. It's green. And they have sexy accents.

Why? Where would you go?

LINA. France.

MAYA. Why?

LINA. I don't know. Looks pretty I guess.

MAYA. Have you ever been?

LINA. No. I've never been to Europe.

MAYA. Seriously?

LINA. Yeah.

MAYA. France is OK. They kinda treat you like shit.

Now how would you feel about some makeup?

LINA. No, I look terrible with makeup.

MAYA. Come on! Please. Just a tiny bit.

LINA. ...

MAYA. Just your eyes.

LINA. Okay.

MAYA. Yay!

> (**MAYA** *begins to choose and apply the makeup.* **LINA** *feels very awkward.*)

Can I ask you a question?

LINA. Sure.

MAYA. Are you gay?

LINA. What?

MAYA. Are you a lesbian?

LINA. Why would you ask that?

MAYA. It's totally fine if you are.

LINA. I'm not. Not at all.

MAYA. I'm just saying that if you are then that's OK, like I just want to make sure that you know that –

LINA. I think I should go.

MAYA. No Lina wait. I'm sorry.

It's none of my business, I shouldn't have asked. I'm sorry.

LINA. Why did you ask?

MAYA. I don't know. I just thought you might be and I want people to feel like they can be themselves with me.

LINA. Are you a lesbian?

MAYA. No.

LINA. How do you know?

MAYA. I've... done stuff with women and I prefer men.

LINA. You've done stuff with women?

MAYA. Yeah a bit... like some kissing and touching.

LINA. When? Where?

MAYA. Are you sure you're not gay?

LINA. Stop!

MAYA. I'm sorry, I'll stop.

Umm... I think it was here. I was fifteen? It was during a sleepover with a friend.

LINA. Was it just that one time?

MAYA. Just that one time. Then we pretended nothing had happened and that was that.

LINA. Wow... I never met anyone whose done anything... like that before.

MAYA. Have you ever done anything, you know, sexual?

LINA. No...

MAYA. Nothing at all?

LINA. *(Shakes her head.)*

MAYA. What about... you know?

LINA. ... I don't know.

MAYA. You and yourself?

LINA. What?

MAYA. Have you ever touched yourself down there?

LINA. No of course not! Do girls really do that here?

MAYA. How old are you?

LINA. Seventeen.

MAYA. And you still haven't touched yourself?

LINA. No! Why would I?

MAYA. It's fun.

LINA. I don't understand why people do that.

MAYA. For the orgasms.

LINA. Are they really that good?

MAYA. Are they... Yes, Lina, yes they are that good.

> (**LINA** *is stunned and awkward and doesn't
> really know what to do or say.*)

LINA. What does it feel like?

MAYA. What do you mean?

LINA. What do... orgasms... feel like?

MAYA. It's like... a wave?

LINA. A wave?

MAYA. I don't know! No one's asked me to describe one
before.

LINA. How do you know if you've had one?

MAYA. Oh you'll definitely know.

LINA. Aren't you scared?

MAYA. Of what?

LINA. What people think?

MAYA. People are wrong.

LINA. Does your family know you have sex?

MAYA. No, of course my family don't know. Who talks to
their family about sex?

And I haven't actually had sex, I'm still a virgin.

LINA. You're still a virgin?

MAYA. Surprising I know.

LINA. But you said you've done stuff... touching.

MAYA. Touching isn't full sex.

LINA. What does that mean?

MAYA. Full sex is you... you know.

LINA. People touching your... is not sex?

MAYA. Look, there's like... different stages.

LINA. Sorry. I just don't know much about... all that.

MAYA. I'm done. What do you think?

> (**MAYA** *steps back to appreciate her craftsmanship.*)

LINA. I look like a doll.

MAYA. Do you like it?

LINA. Umm... yeah. It feels weird, like my face isn't mine.

MAYA. You're welcome.

LINA. I think you're really brave by the way...

MAYA. I'm not brave. You're the one who said yes to a makeover, you're the brave one here.

LINA. I mean... (*Looks at herself in the mirror.*) yeah, you're right.

MAYA. (*Exaggerated gasp.*) Lina!

What are you doing this weekend?

LINA. I spend Fridays with my family.

MAYA. What about Saturday?

LINA. I'm free yeah. Why?

MAYA. I just got my driver's licence, wanna drive around with me? I need to practice and I don't want to do it on my own.

LINA. Sure. I'd like tha –

MAYA. Oh My God! I love this song!

> (**MAYA** *turns the volume up. Something really cheesy and poppy is playing. Something by Justin Bieber or Taylor Swift maybe.*)
>
> (**MAYA** *starts to dance.*)

Come on, dance!

LINA. No, I can't...

MAYA. Lina, dance with me!

LINA. I don't know how to dance.

MAYA. So what? It's just us. Here, just do what they do in the video.

> (**MAYA** *is getting more and more into it.* **LINA** *starts to imitate the video and/or* **MAYA**.)

Yeahhh! Go Lina! Go Lina!

> (**LINA** *laughs and loosens up. They dance. They are having a great time.*)

Scene Eight

*(The flat in Dokki. **OSMAN** is on his laptop typing. He's tense.)*

THE CITY. When Osman was in high school he had friend called Yousef.

Yousef had a habit of getting high and talking about two things.

Pink Floyd and God.

Osman had no interest in either, but he loved those conversations.

For Yousef, believing in a greater power was believing in humanity.

Religion was a true exploration of trying to understand who we are.

For Osman, God was simply an expression of authoritarianism.

Religion; an opium of the masses.

As for Pink Floyd, Yousef called their music

'The greatest exploration of the human condition.'

He would say that Osman would one day experience the transcendental in one form or another.

Pink Floyd or God.

The words of a true a stoner.

But then

One day

Osman goes through a devastating break up.

The kind of break up that makes you take your mum's car and drive to Sinai in the middle of the night.

His mind full of what ifs and should haves.

And Pink Floyd's *The Final Cut* starts to play.

And suddenly...

Osman bursts into tears.

Not emotional tears.

Transcendental tears.

He drives at high speed, windows down, music at full volume.

And that's how Osman is converted.

He tells Yousef the next time he sees him.

His entry Pink Floyd album is *The Final Cut*.

Yousef listens carefully.

Takes a toke.

And says

'Ooft. *The Final Cut*. That's violent.'

Yousef and Osman aren't friends anymore.

They drifted in university.

That's not true.

They just grew apart.

Just tell the truth.

The revolution broke out.

And Yousef didn't choose Tahrir.

And for the first time in their friendship, Osman couldn't reconcile what he was experiencing in the square with what his friend believed.

That's the truth.

OSMAN. *(Typing.)* Down with military rule. I will always say this. I oppose all forms of fascism; and that includes all military dictatorships that plague our region.

Let us be clear here, this regime has killed and massacred. This regime has hijacked the revolution and its narrative. This regime does not have our interests at heart. This regime does not care. They will continue to kill, and incarcerate, and intimidate, and exile all those who oppose them. All those who debate them. All those who question them. And while I can't ask 'who will hold those who murder us to account?' I will never stop saying 'Down with military rule.'

Down with Islamism. Down with Imperialism. Down with Western greed and exploitation. Down with capitalism. Down with fuck fuck fuck. Fuck.

(**RAFIK** *has walked in.*)

RAFIK. Hey.

OSMAN. Rafik. Sorry I …I didn't see you there.

RAFIK. I wasn't expecting you to be back so soon.

OSMAN. They asked us to leave early.

RAFIK. How is she?

OSMAN. She's doing alright. Thinner. She's started drawing, keeps her occupied.

RAFIK. That's good.

OSMAN. Yeah.

RAFIK. When's the next visit?

OSMAN. Next month.

RAFIK. …

OSMAN. I need to work.

RAFIK. I can see that.

OSMAN. I'm having trouble... finding focus.

RAFIK. Maybe go easy on the whole burn the military to the ground... vibe.

OSMAN. I should have been there. I should have been there with her.

RAFIK. I know. I'm sorry.

OSMAN. It's not your fault.

(Silence.)

RAFIK. I went to the Citadel today.

OSMAN. Yeah?

RAFIK. Yeah. I haven't been there in so long! I went in and told everyone I was related to Salaheddin and this guy was like 'my family worked for your family up until the end, generation after generation' and he invited me for tea, so I went to his house –

OSMAN. Rafik

RAFIK. – and I tried to talk Marx and Lenin to him, real talk, you know like Nina Simone says, but he wasn't interested so then I tried to explain who Nina Simone was, I tried to tell him how she's like Um Kulthum –

OSMAN. Please.

RAFIK. – but he was having none of it. I decided that I should play him one of her songs to show him so he would understand and we would have this special bond, but my phone was dead, so then I started to sing her song –

OSMAN. Rafik please!

RAFIK. – *I Got Life*, you know the one I'm talking about? Like

*(**RAFIK** starts to belt out the song.)*

OSMAN. Right OK. Do your thing.

RAFIK. You know the song?

OSMAN. ...

RAFIK. Sing with me.

>*(**RAFIK** continues singing.)*

Come on Osman!

OSMAN. No.

>*(**RAFIK** continues singing.)*

JUST STOP!

RAFIK. NINA SIMONE OSMAN!

>*(**OSMAN** suddenly gives in and sings the end of the song with **RAFIK**.)*

>*(They end the song and stand in silence for a bit.)*

OSMAN. You should join a band.

RAFIK. I was asked once but I told them I only sing Nina Simone songs.

OSMAN. Ha!

RAFIK. ...

OSMAN. I need to get her out of there.

RAFIK. I know.

OSMAN. I have to.

RAFIK. You will.

Scene Nine

THE CITY. Fear.

We can't talk about this city without talking about fear.

This can be a scary place.

Everywhere is scary.

When you don't know it.

Yeah.

The fear here though.

It feels different.

It's not only scary.

It's also exciting.

It challenges you.

It asks

"What do you want?"

And

"How are you going to get it?"

When the revolution broke out.

There was fear.

The fear was familiar.

The fear made sense.

The fear had a purpose.

What the regime didn't realise was we had grown up with this fear.

This city taught us well.

We knew how fear ultimately reveals what we truly desire.

(A car in Moqattam, **ALIA** *and* **TAMER** *are sitting in the front seat, they're kissing, it looks/feels very passionate and very awkward at the same time.)*

TAMER. Use your tongue a bit more.

*(***ALIA*** is a complicated mixture of delight, discomfort and alertness, she doesn't close her eyes when kissing, she keeps looking about her to make sure no one is watching.)*

*(***TAMER*** tries to fondle her breast from under her shirt.)*

ALIA. Tamer no.

TAMER. OK. Can I touch it from the outside?

(She nods, he starts fondling her from over her shirt, his hands go down to her thigh and she lets him keep his hand there, he starts kissing her neck.)

(She thinks she sees something, she tenses up, sensing this **TAMER** *takes a quick glance around.)*

No one's here. Don't worry. All the lights are off, no one will be able to tell that we're here.

ALIA. I know. It's just... if my... anyone ever –

TAMER. I know. Don't worry, I'm sure we won't get caught. Relax OK?

ALIA. OK.

(They continue making out, it gets more and more intense.)

OK I think I'm ready to do it.

(He stops abruptly.)

TAMER. Really?

(She nods.)

You're amazing.

(He unbuttons his trousers, gives her a kiss, she hesitates.)

It's OK.

(He grabs her hand and slowly leads it towards his crotch, but before her hand even touches him, **ALIA** *screams out.)*

ALIA. I CAN'T! No, I can't. I'm so sorry. I thought I could. But I can't, I can't, I

really can't.

TAMER. Calm down.

ALIA. I really thought I could.

TAMER. That's not a problem. It's fine. We don't need to do it.

ALIA. I really want to, you know?

TAMER. I know.

ALIA. Like I want you to feel good and everything. But I just... I can't. I really, really can't.

TAMER. It's fine. Don't worry about it.

ALIA. It's just I thought I wouldn't have to actually touch it. Like I thought I would just touch it, like from the outside. Like from over the clothes.

TAMER. Was that the problem? You can touch it in whatever way you like. I don't mind at all. Do you want to try again?

ALIA. OK. But don't like... pressure me.

TAMER. Yeah OK. No problem. I won't even hold your hand or anything.

ALIA. OK. I'll do it over your underwear OK? You can keep your trousers unbuttoned.

TAMER. OK, yeah, sure.

> *(She takes a deep breath. She takes a couple of awkward glances at her target.)*

> *(**TAMER** is trying to contain his excitement.)*

> *(She starts to go for it. Finally, she begins to touch him. She keeps surveying the outside.)*

ALIA. Like this?

TAMER. Yeah... that's good.

ALIA. This isn't that bad.

TAMER. Yeah? Do you like it?

ALIA. I don't know, it feels weird. Like it's sort of smaller than I expected.

TAMER. Mmhmm...

ALIA. Are they always sort of on the side like that?

TAMER. Different guys have different types. Yeah, like that. Don't stop.

ALIA. Am I doing it right?

TAMER. You're doing great. You can hold it tighter if you want.

ALIA. Like this?

TAMER. Too tight!

ALIA. Sorry! This better?

TAMER. Yess... Like that.

ALIA. This is actually not that bad.

TAMER. Go faster...

(**ALIA** *is starting to relax.*)

Yeah like that...

ALIA. You're really liking this.

TAMER. Yes... Harde –

(**ALIA** *sees something outside. Panics and squeezes.*)

(**TAMER** *screams out in pain.*)

AAAHHHH Alia! Not that hard!

ALIA. Someone's here! No no no no.

(**TAMER** *is still moaning in pain.*)

Tamer! Someone is coming, stop making so much noise. You said no one was gonna see us! Button your trousers!

TAMER. I'm trying!

ALIA. What are we gonna do? What if it's the police?

TAMER. Sshhh. It's OK. No one saw anything.

ALIA. They don't need to. They can tell. Your bulge needs to go down now!

TAMER. I'm trying! You need to calm down you're freaking me out!

ALIA. I'm going to die.

TAMER. What?

ALIA. What if it's an officer?

TAMER. Relax it's gonna be –

ALIA. He might recognise my name!

TAMER. Why would...? You're not making any –

ALIA. So there's something that we've never spoken about before –

TAMER. OK...

ALIA. So all the men in my family are police officers. Military police, intelligence, they're all... some sort of officer.

>   (**TAMER** *takes a moment for that piece of information to sink in.*)

TAMER. WHAT?

ALIA. I didn't know how to tell you.

TAMER. You waited till now to tell me that your family are all –

ALIA. I thought we weren't gonna last, you know? I mean, like how was this supposed to last? It didn't seem like an important –

TAMER. Alia we've been together for two years! I'm head over heels for you, you could have said "oh by the way, my entire family can have you disappeared just like that" –

ALIA. They wouldn't do that.

TAMER. They're gonna chop my dick off, right? Chop it off and feed it to some rabid animal before my eyes –

ALIA. Tamer enough with the drama.

TAMER. – then he'll film it, and put it on YouTube. That's what they do right?

ALIA. That's not –

TAMER. I don't think I could live without a penis. I mean, it's technically doable, but I'm really don't –

ALIA. Maybe it's not a policeman.

TAMER. I'm gonna die.

ALIA. Ok no, it's a policeman.

TAMER. I can't believe this is the way I'm gonna go. I'm gonna die a virgin.

ALIA. No Tamer –

TAMER. And blue-balled! A virgin and blue-balled! How can this be happening to me?

ALIA. TAMER SHUT UP AND CALM DOWN. No one is gonna touch your...thingy!

TAMER. You enjoyed it right? Please don't let my last –

ALIA. You need to bribe him.

TAMER. I ...right, OK. How much money do we have?

ALIA. I've got a couple of twenties.

TAMER. Uhh...so about fifty pounds in total. That won't be enough will it?

ALIA. It'll have to do.

> (**ALIA** *starts to change her appearance slightly.*)

TAMER. Right OK. We've got this. I can do this.

ALIA. We cannot give him my ID, do you understand?

TAMER. Yes. Don't worry. If anything happens, I've got a lawyer friend who can –

ALIA. Tamer don't tell me about your lawyer friend, I cannot get caught like this. You need to make this work, you understand what I'm saying?

TAMER. Yes. I think so.

I can't believe this is happening.

ALIA. You're the one who said no one would find us!

TAMER. I –

ALIA. Go!

(**TAMER** *gets out of the car.*)

Please don't be one of Baba's men. Please god, I will never touch another penis again, I promise, just let him leave us alone.

Scene Ten

*(**MAYA** and **LINA** are in a car parked in the dark. **LINA** is leaning against the hood, **MAYA** starts throwing up in her bag.)*

LINA. Hey, easy there. Just get it all out, that's fine.

MAYA. I'm so sorry Lina, I don't know what happened.

LINA. It's fine. You just had too much to drink, you're fine.

MAYA. I ... I don't... I ...

*(**MAYA** begins to cry.)*

LINA. It's fine. Don't worry about it.

MAYA. But... But Shady...

LINA. Forget him.

MAYA. I ... I thought... Asshole...

(She throws up some more.)

LINA. He was being an idiot. Don't worry about it.

MAYA. But why doesn't he like me...?

LINA. Fuck him.

MAYA. Yes. Fuck him... fuck him... I hate him –

LINA. Now time to go inside alright?

MAYA. I just need to lie down...

LINA. No no... let's go to your room, it's just a few steps away...

*(**MAYA** has already passed out in the back seat of the car.)*

Maya? Come on... Get up! Maya?

*(**LINA** gets her phone out and sends a text. She checks to see if anyone is looking. She lights up a cigarette. She inhales, she coughs. She's not a smoker.)*

Damn it Maya!

Why do you have to be like this?

And why did you kiss that girl? For Shady?

And I thought you were genuinely cool. I thought you knew yourself and what you wanted, but you're just like everyone else.

Trying to attract the attention of complete douchebags.

I HATE going to those parties with you.

You know what else I hate? I hate being your third wheel. I hate hearing about you make out or have not-sex or whatever. I hate lying to your mom when she calls and asks about you, I hate that I have to drive you home all the time and you know that I don't have a licence. Next time I'm leaving you here, passed out in the car, maybe then you'd learn your lesson. Why do I have to be the one to deal with all this? Why do I have to deal with the all the scary shit? You put yourself in danger, no you put US in danger and then I have to get us out of it.

Not anymore. I'm not doing this again. I'm done taking care of you, because you do nothing for me.

A couple of lined eyes and some skinny jeans isn't enough to make me feel good. You didn't even do it because you actually liked me. You did it for yourself. Like you do everything for yourself. Everything!

What about what I want huh? Yeah, what about me, have you ever thought of that? No. Because you are a selfish asshole. Maybe I want to do something different like, like... like go ice skating. Or like have a movie night and make popcorn and, and – and stay in my pyjamas all day. Or maybe, maybe I want to drive to the beach and put my feet in the sand and eat some fish and talk about...talk about...aarrgghhh I can't even think of anything fun because of you!

I'm done. I'm done with this... with this... BULLSHIT!

And I know that you can't hear any of this right now. But I'm gonna be repeating all this. Tomorrow. When you're sober. And conscious.

I swear I'll do it this time.

> (**LINA** *finishes her cigarette. She looks around for something to do. She grabs* **MAYA**'s *bag full of vomit and begins to clean it.*)

Why do you even like any of them?

Why do you want them to like you? What do you get out of it?

Aaagghhh... I hate how much this bothers me!

Bet you'd love it.

Dick.

> (**LINA** *takes her jacket off and covers* **MAYA** *with it.* **LINA** *goes back to cleaning the vomit filled bag. She always alert, always on the lookout.*)

Scene Eleven

(In a café somewhere in **THE CITY**. **RAFIK** *is sitting down, reading a book.* **ALIA** *is just about to leave but notices* **RAFIK**.)*

ALIA. Would you rather have smelly feet or smelly breath for the rest of your life?

RAFIK. *(Takes a moment to recognise who it is.)* Alia!

Come here, give me a hug.

(They hug.)

ALIA. You didn't answer the question.

RAFIK. Smelly feet. Obviously.

ALIA. Still the same as always.

RAFIK. Yup. What about you? Still failing maths?

ALIA. Shut up. Ms. Maha had it in for me and you know it.

RAFIK. Oh yeah, she definitely hated you.

ALIA. Stop!

RAFIK. OK. Truce?

ALIA. Truce.

RAFIK. It's very nice to see you.

ALIA. It's been a good while, hasn't it?

RAFIK. Years.

ALIA. I saw you on TV actually.

RAFIK. On TV?

ALIA. Yes. In Tahrir, you were being interviewed.

RAFIK. Ah... that TV.

ALIA. I didn't know you were political now.

RAFIK. We're all political now, didn't you hear? We had this revolution a few years –

ALIA. You should be careful.

RAFIK. ...

ALIA. Sorry. I don't mean to... sorry.

RAFIK. What about you? Are you political?

ALIA. No...

RAFIK. That's good. Smart.

So how are you? Achieving all your teenage plans? What was it again? Engineering degree by twenty one, engaged by twenty three, married to nice Muslim man by twenty five, first kid by twenty eight? Was that it?

ALIA. I can't believe you remember that.

RAFIK. You on track then?

ALIA. I'm getting the engineering degree...

RAFIK. But no man?

ALIA. No... there's a man.

RAFIK. So you are on track! Impressive.

ALIA. Umm... the man situation is... complicated.

RAFIK. What do you mean?

ALIA. ...

RAFIK. *(Realises what she means.)* No, Alia!

ALIA. Yup...

RAFIK. What is it with you and Christian boys?

ALIA. It's not on purpose!

RAFIK. You can't keep breaking our hearts like that!

ALIA. I didn't break your heart!

RAFIK. Of course you did.

ALIA. Stop it, we only dated for a month.

RAFIK. A month is forever at fifteen.

ALIA. You're right... as usual.

RAFIK. Well... will he convert?

ALIA. I don't know... my father would never accept him I think. And his family are... traditional.

RAFIK. Oh Alia...

ALIA. I know, I know...

Why does it have to be so hard?

RAFIK. You must love the drama.

ALIA. I don't, I swear!

RAFIK. If it all goes to shit, then you can always run away.

ALIA. Yeah right. Where to?

RAFIK. ... Cyprus.

ALIA. Why Cyprus?

RAFIK. You don't need a visa for Cyprus.

ALIA. Really?

RAFIK. Google it.

ALIA. I will. *(She googles.)* And you are... full of *(Lowers voice.)* shit!.

RAFIK. Alia language please.

ALIA. I wish Cyprus was a possibility. I really do.

RAFIK. I wish that too.

(A quiet little moment.)

Seriously though Alia, can you do me a favour?

ALIA. Anything.

RAFIK. Let the boy down gently.

THE CITY. Rafik's first sexual experience with a man happened around the tenth day of the occupation of Tahrir.

That type of experience.

The type of experience where it's literally life or death.

The type of experience that is utterly surreal.

It makes people extra vulnerable.

Rafik was recovering in one of those flats that were open to protestors.

And this person walks in.

They lock eyes and Rafik feels it.

That kick in the stomach.

And he doesn't quite know whether to trust this feeling.

I mean, I don't know if you've ever been involved in a life or death fight for social justice, but it makes people so fucking... sexy.

Or maybe it was all the tear gas he'd inhaled, making him feel woozy.

Or maybe he was just drained and exhausted and this man's beautiful eyes made him feel good.

At the end of the day, it doesn't really matter.

What mattered was that Rafik got up and followed him to the balcony.

They shared a cigarette.

They chatted about the events of the day.

They chatted about what they thought would happen next.

They fell silent for moment that seemed to stretch far and wide and forever.

And Rafik was sure everyone could hear the sound coming from his heart beating so hard.

Then it happened.

They kissed.

There on that balcony.

In the middle of a life-changing revolution.

The square below them, full of life and song and community.

And Rafik could swear fireworks went off the moment it happened.

It was perfect.

Like a film.

Like a dream.

Except it was real.

In this city, these things matter.

Scene Twelve

(The Dokki flat. **MAYA** *and* **RAFIK** *are sitting on the sofa, they're watching* Titanic.*)*

RAFIK. Would you rather watch your lover freeze to death or burn to death?

MAYA. That's a tough one.

I think... I think freeze to death.

RAFIK. Why?

MAYA. So that I don't smell... you know... the burning flesh.

RAFIK. That's fucked.

MAYA. You asked!

RAFIK. You didn't have to answer!

MAYA. You're a prick.

(He lights a joint.)

Can I have a puff?

RAFIK. No.

MAYA. Why not?

RAFIK. Because you're a child.

MAYA. You think this is my first time?

RAFIK. I am a guest in your brother's house, what would he say if he found out?

MAYA. Emphasis on 'if.'

Come on, is it better that I did it elsewhere?

RAFIK. OK... one puff.

And don't tell Osman.

MAYA. Promise.

> *(She takes a big puff and holds it in for as long as she can.)*

RAFIK. Would you rather be with someone kind or someone that can cheer you up?

MAYA. Someone cheerful.

RAFIK. If you had to choose, would you rather be emotionally stable or intelligent?

MAYA. Intelligent, obviously. You?

RAFIK. I can't imagine what being emotionally stable is like.

MAYA. I can't imagine any Egyptian being emotionally stable.

> *(They burst out in stoned laughter. Sound of keys.* **MAYA** *is in a moment of stoned panic, trying to seem normal.)*

RAFIK. Shit.

> *(***OSMAN*** *walks in.)*

Heyyy!

OSMAN. What are you doing here?

MAYA. What? Can't I come visit my dear brother?

OSMAN. You should go.

MAYA. No! The ship... the ship... it's still sinking!

> *(***RAFIK*** *and* **MAYA** *burst out laughing.)*

OSMAN. Are you high?

MAYA. No...

OSMAN. You're fucking high.

RAFIK. Busted.

(**RAFIK** and **MAYA** burst out laughing again.)

OSMAN. What is wrong with you? She's seventeen!

MAYA. I'm eighteen actually.

RAFIK. It was just one puff, and don't tell me you didn't smoke at eighteen.

MAYA. Exactly. Why is it OK for you and not for me? Is it because I'm a girl?

OSMAN. Unbelievable.

RAFIK. I didn't expect you to be home so early.

OSMAN. I'm sorry to barge in on you in my own home.

RAFIK. I'm sorry man... I ... I'm sorry.

OSMAN. You need to leave. Call an uber now.

RAFIK. You can't put her in an uber in this state.

OSMAN. Which is why you're going with her.

MAYA. No. I'm not leaving.

OSMAN. Maya. I'm serious.

MAYA. No.

OSMAN. I'm not fucking about right now.

MAYA. Why can't I stay here? I came to see you and now you're asking me to leave, as usual.

RAFIK. Just let her stay a bit longer.

OSMAN. Stay out of this.

MAYA. I'm not leaving. Besides I can't walk right now.

OSMAN. I can't believe this is happening right now. This is the last thing I need.

RAFIK. She'll be fine by the time Leo sinks into the Atlantic.

MAYA. What's the big deal? I smoke all the time.

OSMAN. Clearly.

Whose shit did she smoke?

RAFIK. The usual.

OSMAN. Mido? You gave my sister dirty hash?

MAYA. What's the difference between dirty hash and clean hash?

OSMAN. I thought you smoked all the time.

MAYA. I do.

OSMAN. I need a shower. Then I'm taking you home.

(**OSMAN** *walks out the room.*)

MAYA. He is not happy.

RAFIK. He's stressed.

MAYA. Is he going to be OK?

RAFIK. I hope so.

MAYA. Me too.

RAFIK. I wish he'd take a break from writing. From ranting.

MAYA. Why?

RAFIK. Umm maybe because it's really dangerous right now.

MAYA. But... we need to tell tyrants to fuck off.

RAFIK. But they don't fuck off do they?

MAYA. One of them did.

RAFIK. But they just keep coming back!

MAYA. Like cockroaches.

RAFIK. What tyrant are we on now? Fourth? Fifth? Hundredth? Five hundredth?

MAYA. I don't know...

RAFIK. Which one do you think is the first one? Are the pharaohs considered tyrants?

MAYA. They must have been.

Ramsis II was a tyrant. Like in the Quran. And the Bible... they were definitely tyrants. They must have been.

RAFIK. You know what fascinates me? People believing Moses was real, in the literal sense. I mean, they say he drowned a pharaoh's entire army in the red sea, right? That he brought on a plague and did all sorts of crazy shit, and the ancient Egyptians, the ones that literally recorded everything, were like... let's just leave that part out. Why would they do that?

MAYA. You sound like my brother.

RAFIK. Shit... I totally sound like him. I don't know how I feel about that.

(**MAYA** *begins to pass out.*)

No no no, you need to stay awake so you can go home.

MAYA. I think... I think I'm just gonna take a nap.

(**RAFIK** *tries to revive her but has no luck. He then takes out* **OSMAN***'s laptop, takes a moment to make sure* **OSMAN** *is still in the shower. He goes through the laptop and starts to delete drafts blog posts and articles. He then puts the laptop back by the time* **OSMAN** *comes back into the room.*)

OSMAN. You're joking.

RAFIK. I tried to stop her, I swear.

OSMAN. Sure you did.

MAYA. *(Still in a stupor.)* I'm fine. I just need to lie down for a while.

OSMAN. Help me move her to the bed at least.

> (**RAFIK** *and* **OSMAN** *gently revive* **MAYA** *and carry her out.*)

Scene Thirteen

THE CITY.   When the revolution broke out. Maya was thirteen.

Because of how active her family was, she spent much of it with her aunts and uncles and cousins, watching it on TV.

Everyone decided that she should be kept sheltered from it.

Which is super weird.

She wasn't that young.

They could have asked her.

But as usual they didn't.

Maya has always felt like she was treated like an idiot by both her parents.

As for Osman.

He pretty much ignored her.

He became wrapped up in becoming the next Che Guevara.

She felt he was patronising.

Politics is what brought her parents together.

But they didn't stay together long.

And Maya always felt that politics is what tore her family apart.

Her father carried a lot of anger.

And a lot of pain.

And so he drank.

And so he deflected and projected and ignored.

Are we being fair though?

Yes.

He fucked things up.

And for years Maya carried a lot of that pain, and a lot of that anger.

And she decided that every decision she makes would be done so fully.

She was not going to be like her father.

She was not going to be like her brother.

She was going to be happy.

She was going to live life fully.

Regardless of all the failed revolutions.

She didn't want to spend her life fighting for a place that did not think twice about crushing her.

> (**MAYA** *and* **LINA** *are in a car blasting something dancey like a song in the style of Rihanna's* **["WE FOUND LOVE"]**. *They get stuck in traffic on the 6th of October bridge.* **MAYA** *is dancing and singing along with her entire body.* **LINA** *is more subdued bobbing her head along but enjoying the outrageousness of* **MAYA**.)

> (*Suddenly* **MAYA** *notices that they're being watched.*)

MAYA. The fuck you looking at.

LINA. Maya stop. No, stop it.

Just let it go.

MAYA. I hate it when they stare.

LINA. It's gross. But responding just makes it worse.

MAYA. What time is it?

LINA. It's nine.

MAYA. Come on! We're gonna be late.

Don't you people know we've got places to be! And Lina has a curfew, we can't waste our time here.

LINA. ...

MAYA. What's wrong? Why so quiet?

LINA. No reason.

MAYA. I'm bursting for a pee.

Come on! For the love of God, MOVE!

Fuck you Cairo!

Yeah you! And you! And most definitely YOU!

LINA. That's not going to help.

MAYA. Can you take the wheel for a sec?

LINA. Why?

MAYA. I don't think we have time to stop at mine.

(**MAYA** *gets into the back seat.*)

LINA. Maya no. I'm not doing this again. I'm not getting behind the wheel.

MAYA. OK, just leave the seat empty then, it'll only take a second and it doesn't look like we'll be moving any time soon.

LINA. Maya please, come back, you can change when we get there.

MAYA. I'm not arriving at a party dressed like this.

LINA. I hate you.

MAYA. You love me.

(**LINA** *climbs into the front seat.*)

Thank you Luli.

LINA. Stop calling me that.

(**MAYA** *gives* **LINA** *a kiss on the cheek.*)

Are you seriously gonna change here on the bridge?

MAYA. No one will see I promise.

LINA. Mayyaa...

MAYA. Linnaa... Relax, I've done this a thousand times.

(She begins to change in the backseat and then starts to apply makeup.)

Who do you think will be there? Do you think there'll be someone exciting, someone I can flirt with –

LINA. I don't want to go to this party.

MAYA. What? Why?

LINA. I hate the parties you go to. The people are always weird.

MAYA. But I need you there.

LINA. Why do you need me there? You always leave me the second we arrive.

MAYA. That's not true!

LINA. It is. You always go off and make out with someone or whatever.

MAYA. I'm just enjoying myself, it's not serious or anything. And I never leave for that long.

LINA. I don't like you making out with those guys.

MAYA. Why not? They're fun.

LINA. They're creeps.

MAYA. What's wrong with you?

LINA. I ... I'm just don't like them. Guys that age shouldn't be hanging out around people our age. They're slimey.

MAYA. Why didn't you say something earlier?

LINA. I didn't want to hurt your feelings.

MAYA. Do you really think Shady is slimey?

LINA. Maya, he's revolting.

MAYA. But I liked him...

LINA. We need to set some standards. You can do so much better.

MAYA. You're still going to come, you can't let me go to this party on my own.

LINA. Maya... I don't –

MAYA. Pleeeease. I need someone to get drunk with.

LINA. Remember last time?

MAYA. Exactly. You took such good care of me.

LINA. I'm not coming.

MAYA. I need you.

LINA. Nope.

MAYA. I promise not to leave you.

LINA. I'm going home.

MAYA. If you don't come I'm gonna pee in this car right now.

LINA. Whatever.

MAYA. You don't believe me?

LINA. What are you doing?

MAYA. I'm absolutely dying to pee, I'm just going to have to do it here.

LINA. No!

MAYA. You know I'm going to do it.

LINA. Maya you can't!

MAYA. I think I have the right to pee in my own car.

LINA. MAYA!

MAYA. I'm doing it.

LINA. Alright! Stop! I'll come with you.

MAYA. You promise?

LINA. Promise! I promise!

MAYA. Yes!

LINA. Traffic's moving.

> (**MAYA** *quickly climbs back into the front seat, she gestures aggressively to the car next to them.*)

MAYA. What? Assholes.

Should we race them?

LINA. With this piece of junk?

MAYA. Don't call Marzouk a piece of junk!

She didn't mean it baby.

LINA. Come on Marzouk please get us there in one piece.

MAYA. Marzouk has never let us down.

LINA. ...

MAYA. What? Oh come on, he just needed a little push.

LINA. You're doing the pushing next time.

MAYA. I love having adventures with you.

LINA. ...

MAYA. Lina!

LINA. OK fine. I also love our adventures.

MAYA. Yaay!

> *(They blast the music as they drive off to their next adventure.)*

Scene Fourteen

(TAMER and ALIA are in a dark staircase of a building. She's pressed up against the walk, TAMER has his hand up her skirt, they're kissing. As usual ALIA is looking about.)

ALIA. This is really risky Tamer.

TAMER. You want me to stop?

ALIA. No.

I don't know.

(She moans. TAMER puts his free hand over her mouth.)

TAMER. Sshhh... I love you.

ALIA. I love you too.

(They kiss. TAMER becomes overzealous.)

Oww... Stop, stop.

(TAMER removes his hand, it's covered in blood.)

TAMER. Oh no! Oh shit! You're bleeding! Shit, shit!

ALIA. Sshhh... Tamer calm –

TAMER. Shit Alia! I didn't mean it! How did I hurt you so bad?

ALIA. I don't know. It didn't really hurt.

TAMER. Why are you bleeding?

ALIA. I think it might be –

TAMER. Is it your period?

ALIA. No, it's not my –

TAMER. Didn't it just end? What should we do?

ALIA. Tamer –

TAMER. Do I take you to the hospital? What are we gonna tell them?

ALIA. Tamer! I think that was my hymen.

TAMER. You mean –

ALIA. You probably broke my hymen.

TAMER. So...

ALIA. I'm not...

TAMER. I'm so sorry Alia. I'm so so sorry. I didn't mean to take your virginity, I swear. I didn't think it could happen with a finger.

ALIA. I can't believe I'm not a virgin anymore.

TAMER. I'm sure we can find a way to fix this.

ALIA. I lost my virginity...

TAMER. No –

ALIA. Before marriage...

TAMER. We haven't had sex, so you're still –

ALIA. To a finger!

TAMER. I ... I'm – I ... We... We can –

ALIA. What am I gonna do?!

TAMER. It's fine, it doesn't count!

ALIA. It's my hymen Tamer! I don't have another one do I?

TAMER. You can have that operation.

ALIA. What?

TAMER. The one that makes you a virgin again.

ALIA. What?

TAMER. I'm sure we can find a doctor that's you know...
cool.

ALIA. You want me to have surgery?

TAMER. I don't know, I just... I don't know about these
things.

ALIA. I was so careful. So so careful.

TAMER. What about that portable Chinese hymen thing?

ALIA. What Chinese hymen thing?

TAMER. The one on the internet.

ALIA. Can you hear yourself right now?

TAMER. There were pictures of it all over Facebook. It's
like a hymen in a box. And it's Chinese so it's bound to
be cheaper than –

ALIA. Hymen in a box from China?

TAMER. Yeah...

ALIA. You want me to buy a hymen from China and then
stick it up my –

TAMER. I'm not exactly sure how it works but –

ALIA. Stop. Stop talking. I am not inserting anything up
there ever again! I knew I shouldn't have listened to
you...

(**ALIA** *sits on a step and begins to cry.*)

TAMER. No. Please don't cry I'm sorry. Shhh...

ALIA. I knew it was a mistake. How am I gonna have a
future? Everyone will know...

TAMER. No one will know.

ALIA. First I lose my virginity and what next? Pregnancy?

TAMER. Alia calm down, people will hear.

ALIA. I'm ruined.

TAMER. You're not ruined.

ALIA. I didn't even do what the other girls do. I've never
given head to anyone. No one saw me naked. I didn't
even have sex! What am I gonna do?

TAMER. Why don't we get married?

ALIA. Tamer be serious.

TAMER. I am. I've never been more serious.

Marry me.

ALIA. How?

TAMER. I'll convert.

ALIA. What about our families?

TAMER. Fuck our families!

ALIA. This is crazy.

TAMER. Is that a yes?

ALIA. It's impossible for us to marry here.

TAMER. Then let's... then maybe we can...

ALIA. Leave.

TAMER. What?

ALIA. Let's leave Egypt.

> (*A noise is heard, someone has entered the
> building.*)

Run to the roof, I'll meet you on the corner, in front of
Costa.

TAMER. Right.

> (**TAMER** *leans in for a kiss.*)

ALIA. Seriously?

TAMER. Right, sorry, see you in a bit!

Scene Fifteen

(**MAYA**'s room. **LINA** is looking through a magazine, while **MAYA** is texting. **MAYA** finishes her text and tries to get **LINA**'s attention. **LINA** ignores her.)

MAYA. Lina!

LINA. What?

MAYA. I need to tell you something.

LINA. OK.

MAYA. First of all. I've been seeing someone.

LINA. What?

MAYA. We've been keeping it kind of secret.

LINA. Why? Wait what is going on, who is this person?

MAYA. Amir

LINA. Who the fuck is Amir?

MAYA. Remember the guy I was flirting with at the Mansoura party?

LINA. You're going to have to be more specific than that.

MAYA. The tall guy.

LINA. ...

MAYA. He bought us shots.

LINA. ...

MAYA. He had an awkward friend with him, with a Metallica t-shirt. You guys seemed to get along.

LINA. The guy who kept patting me on the head?

MAYA. I think he was trying to flirt with you.

LINA. THAT guy's friend? The one with the FEDORA?

MAYA. Yeah, Amir.

LINA. I can't believe you're seeing Mr. Fedora.

MAYA. What's wrong with him?

LINA. His dress sense for one!

MAYA. Look who's talking.

LINA. Isn't he like forty?

MAYA. Stop being so dramatic, he's twenty three.

LINA. That's old!

MAYA. Twenty three isn't old. Stop making such a big deal about this.

LINA. How long has this been going on?

MAYA. Well… since that party, so like two or three months?

LINA. Why didn't you tell me?

MAYA. I'm telling you now.

LINA. I can't believe this.

MAYA. I haven't even finished what I wanted to say!

LINA. There's more??

MAYA. Yes.

LINA. I don't know if I can take any more to be honest.

MAYA. He wants to take me to Ras Sedr for the weekend, his family has a house there.

LINA. Are you gonna go?

MAYA. Yes. And… we're going to have sex there.

LINA. …

MAYA. Lina say something.

LINA. Like actual sex?

MAYA. Like actual sex.

LINA. Are you fucking kidding me?

MAYA. What?

LINA. What is happening right now? I feel like the whole world is imploding.

MAYA. Why?

LINA. I can't believe this. I can't believe you've been dating creepy fedora man and now you want to lose your virginity to him, like an idiot.

MAYA. I'm not an idiot.

LINA. Yes you are. Who even is this creep?

MAYA. Stop saying he's a creep, I actually really like this guy. I think I might actually be in love with him.

LINA. Wow. In love? OK. This is just great.

MAYA. What's your problem?

LINA. My problem is that you've fallen in love, and didn't tell me, and I'm supposedly your best friend. And you're about to make a massive mistake.

MAYA. Why is this a mistake? I want this Lina.

LINA. You live in Egypt Maya, there's no going back. Why do you keep doing this?

MAYA. Doing what?

LINA. You're going to be ruined.

MAYA. Why are you being a total dick right now?

LINA. Just because I fucking care doesn't make me a dick.

MAYA. If you fucking cared then you would be supporting me. Come with me to buy condoms, that sort of thing.

LINA. Oh he's making you buy the condoms? What a gentleman.

MAYA. Of course he's buying the condoms! I was just making a point.

LINA. Why him?

MAYA. What do you mean?

LINA. Why him? Out of all the people you've been with, why him?

MAYA. I don't know. I just... he makes me feel special.

LINA. And no one else made you feel special?

MAYA. That's not... I don't know, it's different this time.

LINA. It's your virginity, you don't have another one.

MAYA. I know that I –

LINA. You need to start thinking about your reputation.

MAYA. Since when do you care about my reputation?

LINA. I'm just worried about you.

MAYA. Don't be. People here have sex all the time Lina –

LINA. Who do you know that has had sex?

MAYA. Well...

LINA. Exactly.

MAYA. Tanya!

LINA. You want to end up like Tanya? She almost got disowned by her family.

MAYA. My mother wouldn't do that.

LINA. If people find out they're gonna talk, and it's not just about you, they're going to talk about your mother as well, imagine what it'll do to her reputation as a professor, as a writer?

MAYA. People talk anyway, what's the big deal?

LINA. What if you get pregnant? What if you get a disease, what then? What are you gonna do?

MAYA. I'll figure it out.

LINA. What if you break up after you have sex?

MAYA. Lina enough. I want to have sex. I want it to be OK for women in this country to have sex whenever and however they want. What's the point of me saying all the stuff that I say if I don't live it as well?

LINA. Don't you think sex is going to change everything? Do you really think he'll respect you after you do this?

MAYA. Why wouldn't he respect me?

LINA. Men do that. They fuck around and then marry the good virgin girl, everyone knows that.

Just please don't do it!

MAYA. Why are you –

LINA. He's bad news Maya please listen to me –

MAYA. No, he's not.

LINA. Stop bullshitting yourself!

MAYA. I'm not.

LINA. Yes you are!

MAYA. No I'm not! You're the one who's just being a fucking bitch right now!

LINA. I'm not the bitch!

MAYA. Yes you are!

LINA. No I'm not. You are. You're the fucking bitch!

MAYA. Well if I'm a bitch then why are you here?

LINA. Why do you feel the need to act like a slut just to feel liberated!

MAYA. Woah. Wow, OK.

LINA. Sorry, that – I, that's not.

MAYA. Is that what you really think of me?

LINA. No, that's not what I meant! I just –

MAYA. You know what? I don't care.

LINA. Please Maya –

MAYA. I've had enough of this, just take your dried up pussy and fuck off!

LINA. What did you just call my pussy?

MAYA. It's dried up and joyless, just like you.

LINA. Maya! Stop –

MAYA. I'm such an idiot. I actually BELIEVED that you were my friend, but you're just like the rest of them, jealous, joyless, full of resentment because I actually want to live as I –

LINA. MAYA JUST SHUT THE FUCK UP. I LOVE YOU, OK?

> *(Stunned silence.)*

I don't want you having sex with that guy or anyone else... because I think...

I think I'm in love with you.

MAYA. But you said...

LINA. I know what I said.

MAYA. I'm not gay.

LINA. I'm... I'm sorry.

I need to go.

> *(**LINA** leaves.)*

Scene Sixteen

(The Dokki flat. **RAFIK** *is sitting on the couch. He's smoking.* **OSMAN** *is on his laptop. Things feel tense.)*

RAFIK. Would you rather have a difficult life but be with someone who loves and supports you or have an easy life and be alone?

OSMAN. ...

RAFIK. Do you want to order some food?

OSMAN. ...

RAFIK. Osman?

OSMAN. Did you go through my laptop?

RAFIK. What?

OSMAN. You heard me.

RAFIK. Maybe it's one of those creepy hackers that get your laptop and makes it seem like it's haunted.

OSMAN. Rafik, I'm not joking.

RAFIK. So am I!

OSMAN. I'm being completely serious right now, and I need you to answer me. Genuinely.

RAFIK. ...

OSMAN. I'm going to ask you one more time.

Did you go through my laptop?

RAFIK. ...

OSMAN. Answer me.

RAFIK. No.

*(**OSMAN** suddenly grabs **RAFIK**'s phone.)*

RAFIK. Osman...

OSMAN. DID YOU DELETE MY WORK OR NOT?

RAFIK. I couldn't get you to listen.

OSMAN. So you invaded my privacy?

You delete my work, I delete grindr isn't that the deal? So I assume you deleted it... and of course you didn't.

(**OSMAN** *deletes it all.*)

RAFIK. Osman, enough, you've made your point.

OSMAN. You think this is about making a point?

RAFIK. Give it back to me.

OSMAN. I'm not done yet.

RAFIK. Why are you doing this?

OSMAN. Doing what?

RAFIK. ...

OSMAN. What am I doing Rafik?

RAFIK. You're... you're erasing me.

OSMAN. Just like you did to me.

RAFIK. I was erasing your work, it's different.

OSMAN. That is my life!

RAFIK. No. This is about safety, if you actually cared about –

OSMAN. You think I don't care?

RAFIK. What about those that need you right now? What about Zeina?

OSMAN. Don't tell me what Zeina needs.

RAFIK. I've been seeing agents walking outside our building for months now. Your resistance is going to cost Zeina her freedom. It's going to cost you your life.

OSMAN. And your fucking isn't?

RAFIK. ...

You know what?

(**RAFIK** *grabs* **OSMAN**'s *laptop.*)

Fuck your words.

(**RAFIK** *smashes the laptop.*)

OSMAN. What happened to you? Who are you? What happened to... what happened to "we won't stop till this system is dead"?

RAFIK. Don't you see that the system is already dead? It's the fucking undead! You know what'll happen if you keep on writing, you know that, and yet you keep on doing it. Our friends are being thrown into jail, are being disappeared, and you're still writing. What will it take for you to just stop. Just for a bit.

OSMAN. If I don't keep doing this, then they win.

RAFIK. They've already won. Why can't you see that?

OSMAN. I don't believe that! I still think we have a chance, I want to keep fighting. I have to. Why can't you just accept –

RAFIK. Because I'm done with this, alright? I'm done. None of it is worth the risk. All those people who died in the past four years, thinking they were dying for a great cause –

OSMAN. They died believing –

RAFIK. They believed wrong! They died for nothing. Nothing Osman!

The problem isn't the government, it isn't about who's in power or which fascist you want to side with. It's the people. That's the problem. It's us and people like us. It's our comfortable little messed up bubble. The vulnerable are still vulnerable. The poor are still dying. They never stopped dying. They continued dying while we played revolutionaries.

"But they will live on in history!"

Bullshit. They died for nothing. No one will remember them.

OSMAN. How can you say that! They meant something. And we are here to remind everyone of that. To remind them –

RAFIK. Who's everyone? Who Osman? Who is listening that doesn't know all this already? Who is listening at all? We're not making a difference. No one cares anymore. No one cares about us. No one cares about Egypt.

Tahrir is over. It's done. And the sooner you understand this, the sooner we can all move on and maybe get a chance to live something that's a semblance of a bearable life.

OSMAN. ...

RAFIK. ...

OSMAN. Get out.

RAFIK. ...

OSMAN. Get out. Get out of my house!

RAFIK. ...

OSMAN. How dare you. How fucking dare you.

RAFIK. Osman...

OSMAN. How dare you stay in my house and –

RAFIK. Osman please...

OSMAN. NO! YOU DON'T SAY ANOTHER WORD, GET OUT!

RAFIK. You don't mean that.

OSMAN. I can't do this.

RAFIK. ...

OSMAN. I can't do this anymore.

I don't want the life you want for me. I don't want to live in fear. I refuse to live in fear. I'd rather die than live in fear.

RAFIK. ...

OSMAN. I'm tired to explaining myself to you.

I'm done.

You can't stay here anymore. I can't live with you, not when you're like this. I'm barely hanging on myself. I'm barely keeping it together. I need to believe in what I'm doing.

Even if you don't.

I want you out of my life.

RAFIK. Osman...

OSMAN. Please.

RAFIK. ...

OSMAN. Please just go.

RAFIK. ...

OSMAN. ...

RAFIK. Do you really mean that?

OSMAN. Yes.

RAFIK. Alright. I'll leave.

(**RAFIK** *goes into his room and grabs his rucksack. He decides there's nothing else to say. He leaves, slamming the door behind him.*)

THE CITY. The thing about revolution is that it is a live thing.

In the pavement cracks.

In the peeling walls.

In the tarmac, and cement, and mortar.

In the trees, and grass and air.

In its shadows.

It shifts and crackles and rumbles.

As Rafik tries to forget.

Just let him forget!   NO!

This isn't about Tahrir.

Of course it is!   STOP!

As Osman desperately tries to remember every detail.

It will kill him. This will kill him.

You can't stop it.

They can't stop.

These memories are part of us.

WE are the ghosts.

In this city these things matter!

In this city these things happened.

The thing about revolution is...

It's all layers.

(The revolution seeps through the cracks.)

It's bodies and voices.

Louder.

It's marches and chants.

I said louder.

Louder.

LOUDER!   YES!

It's everywhere   Yes!   Over here.

LOUDER!

It's walking into the unknown.

It's seeing rows of riot police and knowing that they might crack your head open.

It's experiencing tear gas for the first time.

INCOMING!

(Tear gas.)

(Tear gas.)   *(Tear gas.)*

(Tear gas.)

It's more tear gas!   Much more.

(Tear gas.)

(Tear gas.)   *(Tear gas.)*   *(Tear gas.)*

(Tear gas.)   *(Tear gas.)*

It's a group of strangers protecting each other.

It's waiting for days.

So much waiting.

It's riot police beating the shit out of us.

It's playing angry birds for days
and days.

It's not having internet for a week.   It's no mobile
network for
twenty four
hours.

It's taking over a square.

That's not even a square.

(Danger.)   It's a roundabout.   *(Danger.)*

And holding on for dear life.

It's makeshift helmets and shields.   It's rocks as
weapons.

And
Molotov
cocktails.

INCOMING!

(Danger.)

TO THE FRONT LINES!

(Danger.)   *(Danger.)*

Injured to the middle of the square!

(Danger.)   *(Danger.)*

(Danger.)

It's fighting off attacks by men on camels and with
machetes and riot police.

It's all the police evacuating the city.   A police
state with
no police.

It's Christians forming a human chain to protect
Muslims during Friday prayer.

| It's long nights guarding your home | It's people being politicised for the first time! | It's long nights of political debates and collective dreams and hope! |

| It's a city getting to know its neighbours for the first time. | It's people seeing their politics make a difference for the first time! | REAL ACTUAL FUCKING HOPE! |

It's waiting.   So much waiting.   Too much waiting.

It's more battles.

THE REVOLUTION   It's not leaving your house
LIVES ON   for days.
COMRADES IN OUR
HEARTS IN OUR
MINDS IN OUR   It's the military planes
MOTHERFUCKING   flying on to the square.
BODIES

(A military plane flies over.)
Lower.
MUCH LOUDER!
(The square is not intimated.)

It's a father asking his daughter to tell him what
she's willing to die for.

INCOMING!

(Tear gas.)

It's tear gas and rubber bullets and water cannons.

It's conspiracy theories and scare tactics and government propaganda.

(Rubber bullet rubber bullets rubber bullets.)

It's tears.

(So many tears.)   And exhaustion.

And fear.

It's depending on the kindness of others.

It's two strangers falling to their knees and praying to a God they don't believe in.

It's a mother screaming out in grief!

(Cries of grief.)

It's cries of war.

(Cries of war.)

Cries of joy!

(Cries of joy.)

It's love

REAL UNADULTERATED LOVE!

AND IT'S POETRY!

AND MUSIC!

AND ART!

AND THEATRE!

It's the military moving into the square.

(The military moves in.)

It's not knowing.

They'regonnakillusthey're gonnakillus

No they're with us. They're with us.

Not knowing

It's that announcement.

(*Omar Soliman's voice announcing that Mubarak will be stepping down.*)

That split second of silence.

Holding my breath.

All of us.

Holding our breath.

(*That split second of silence as the memory of realizing that Mubarak is actually stepping down hits all of them. And all of us.*)

A city on the brink of change.

That's who we were.

For a split second.

That's who they were.

Two revolutionaries, imagining a better tomorrow.

(*The memories are now like ghosts. A haunting. An experience that occupies the space between a dream and a nightmare.*)

Scene Seventeen

*(**RAFIK** walks out into the night. He walks along the Nile and sits on a bench.)*

RAFIK. So what's next? Huh? What delights have you got in store for me, Cairo?

A fun, wholesome adventure by the seaside? Backpacking down the Nile? Living my best boho life like a Brit on their gap year?

THE CITY. …

RAFIK. Since when are you so shy?

THE CITY. You're making fun.

RAFIK. It's what we do, isn't it?

THE CITY. Sometimes.

RAFIK. Even when things are very serious.

THE CITY. Even when things are fucked up.

RAFIK. That's the thing about Cairo… she's all layers.

THE CITY. That's right.

RAFIK. It's true. Sometimes it feels like we're living in several dimensions, all at the same time.

Multitudes.

THE CITY. Do you have a favourite layer?

RAFIK. I like… melancholy. It's romantic. Wouldn't you say I'm romantic?

THE CITY. A bit, yes.

RAFIK. Only a bit? Come on, give me a bit more credit than that.

THE CITY. …

(The silence is heavy.)

RAFIK. They're going to take me, aren't they?

THE CITY. Yes.

RAFIK. What's going to happen to me?

THE CITY. They'll blindfold you and take you away from here.

They'll take your phone and question you.

They'll probably torture you as well.

RAFIK. They do that, don't they?

THE CITY. They do.

Are you scared?

RAFIK. You know, it's strange to say but I don't really feel anything, now that it's happening.

I've been terrified for a long time.

I didn't do anything wrong.

I even tried to keep to myself.

But this isn't about that.

THE CITY. He will blame himself.

RAFIK. He shouldn't. It's not his fault. None of this is his fault. No one did anything wrong.

I shouldn't have said all that to him.

THE CITY. People are clumsy in this city.

Clumsy with their emotions.

Clumsy with their violence.

Tends to just spill over everything.

RAFIK. ...

Am I ever going to be found?

THE CITY. I don't know.

RAFIK. I'm sure someone will.

Even if it's just a corpse.

People don't disappear forever here. Not usually.

THE CITY. No?

RAFIK. You're not great at comfort, you know that?

THE CITY. Even if you disappear forever, they might not stop looking for you.

RAFIK. ...

I didn't even think about that.

THE CITY. ...

RAFIK. That's scary.

THE CITY. They will look for you.

There'll be social media posts and pages and hashtags.

There'll be articles. National ones, then international ones.

International organisations might try to put pressure on the government to reveal your whereabouts.

There might be theories about what happened to you.

There might be conspiracy theories.

People will lose their sleep and their sanity over this.

...

RAFIK. And then?

THE CITY. I don't know.

RAFIK. I don't want them to forget.

THE CITY. ...

RAFIK. Please don't let them forget.

THE CITY. ...

RAFIK. Please don't forget me.

THE CITY. I think it's time.

> (**RAFIK** *gets up. He takes it all in, all of the layers of this city, one last time.*)

RAFIK. God I love this city.

> (**THE CITY** *holds his hand, and together they walk into the darkness.*)

> (**RAFIK** *disappears.*)

Scene Eighteen

THE CITY. And now?

Yeah, now what?

And now Osman...

No!

Now Osman and Maya and Alia and –

I don't want to do this.

But we have to.

They are still part of this city.

It starts with doubt.

It trickles in.

No contact.

No phone.

So is Rafik.

He's still a part of this city.

A call being made.

Have you seen Rafik?

Has anyone seen Rafik?

No.

No.

No.

How long ago was this?

The last time I saw him was three days ago.

Check the hospitals.

I'll check the prisons.

Call the lawyer.

Someone should tell his parents.

#FindRafik

It seeps.

Seeps through the cracks and the ruptures.

An old friend.

A friend of a friend.

A student.

A lover.

An ex-lover.

An acquaintance.

A son.

A brother.

An aspiring novelist.

A poet.

Did he actually write poetry?

He did.

When he was in high school.

He taught me how to imagine.

He taught me how to escape.

He's not at any of the hospitals.

They're saying he's not in the prisons.

So where is he?

They've taken him.

They must have.

Maybe it was a robbery gone wrong?

Another violent crime?

Kidnapped?

He was definitely kidnapped.

Forcibly disappeared.

That's what they call it.

I don't know.

Kidnapped by the state.

We don't know.

They did this, we all know it!

No one knows.

Has anyone seen him?

Has anyone seen anything?

Has anyone seen my friend?

Maybe I could ask my father.

Maybe my cousin can help.

Maybe he ran away?

No.

Don't be naïve.

No one runs away like this.

Please help us find him.

Someone must have seen something.

Someone in this city must have seen something.

This city must know.

It must.

It must –

This city must know and it's fucking with us and it's just finding a way for us to stay tied to it so it can destroy us to punish us to hate us because all this city knows is how to break and smother and destroy and crush and take everything it takes and takes and takes and –

And it loves.

NO.

Yes. It loves fiercely!

Months pass and nothing.

No sign of him.

No word from him.

And Osman?

Nothing.

Osman's lost.

Nothing.

This.

This is not love.

This city does not know how to love.

This city can't love.

It is bruised and broken and shattered.

This city barely exists.

This city is nothing but fragments.

    (**THE CITY** *shatters.*)

Scene Nineteen

> (**MAYA** *is sitting on the roof of the school. It's*
> *the last day of school.* **LINA** *walks in, she sits*
> *with her.*)

MAYA. Can we friends again?

LINA. Is that what you want?

MAYA. Yes. I ...

> (**MAYA** *holds* **LINA**'s *hand. They're quiet for a*
> *moment.*)

LINA. You don't need to –

MAYA. I haven't stopped thinking about you.

LINA. Really?

MAYA. When... I ...since Rafik disappeared, I ...

LINA. Maya...

MAYA. Wait let me finish. I ... It's made me realise that... I
don't want to regret anything. It made me think about
what I want and well...

> *(They're quiet for a bit.)*

LINA. I'm sorry I was such a dick.

MAYA. Who isn't one these days?

> *(They sort of laugh.)*

I've missed you.

LINA. I've missed you too. So much.

I also haven't been able to stop thinking about you.

MAYA. Really?

LINA. Really. I feel like I'm in a cheesy American teen flick.

What am I gonna do? Make a grand reveal to my parents like they do abroad? *(In an exaggerated American accent.)* "Mom. Dad. I think you need to be sitting down for this. I need to tell you something."

My father will ship me off to the first rehab centre for gay people he can find. And this would destroy my mother... Yeah, I can't do that to her.

MAYA. You don't need to tell them. Not now anyway.

LINA. And I keep thinking that this can't be right.

MAYA. This is the only thing that feels right.

LINA. Really?

MAYA. Really.

> *(They're quiet for a second.)*

LINA. I thought you said you're not gay.

MAYA. I thought you said you're not a lesbian.

> *(More gentle awkward laughter.)*

LINA. I don't expect you to be... you know... I don't really expect anything.

MAYA. I don't really know what to expect.

> *(They're quiet for another second.)*

LINA. Wow.

MAYA. Did you just say wow?

LINA. Yeah. Wow.

> *(There's a feeling of nervous tension and quiet anticipation at the same time. They are totally in the moment.)*

I'm scared.

MAYA. Me too.

*(**MAYA** looks around, making sure they can't be seen. **MAYA** kisses **LINA**.)*

LINA. Wow.

*(They look at one another. They laugh. **MAYA** puts her head on **LINA**'s shoulder.)*

Scene Twenty

*(A sports shop in Mohandessin. **TAMER** is looking at inflatable rafts. He looks stressed, he has no idea what he's looking for. He looks for someone to help him out. A lost soul is standing there. It's **OSMAN**.)*

TAMER. Excuse me?

OSMAN. Me?

TAMER. I'm really sorry to bother you, but I was just wondering whether you knew anything about rafts?

OSMAN. You're buying a raft?

TAMER. Yes, I'm... I'm considering it.

OSMAN. They sell rafts here?

TAMER. I mean... it's not a huge selection, a lot of it is for children.

OSMAN. This is a fucking weird shop, isn't it?

TAMER. Sure... if you don't want to buy sports equip –

OSMAN. Like why are they selling skis?? SKIS!

TAMER. That is a bit... strange. Are you alright?

OSMAN. No. No I am not OK. I am not OK with this.

I mean, who is buying this? Is this for the ten rich kids that go skiing in Switzerland every winter? Like what is going on here?

TAMER. I –

OSMAN. Surely they have money to buy their fucking skis in fucking Switzerland.

Know what I mean?

TAMER. Totally, yeah. Are you sure you should be here, you seem... upset.

OSMAN. I'm not upset. I'm just drunk.

I don't even know why I'm here.

I thought I needed something.

I thought... I don't know... I ...

> (**OSMAN** *collapses in tears and* **TAMER** *catches him, and gently holds him on the floor. He looks around, it's unusual for a shop not to have anyone around.*)

TAMER. Hey... It's OK.

OSMAN. I'm a terrible person.

TAMER. I'm... I'm sure you're not.

OSMAN. No, I am.

TAMER. You're just... going through a lot.

OSMAN. I killed my best friend.

TAMER. Like... actually killed him.

OSMAN. With my words.

TAMER. Oh thank god. Words can't kill anyone.

OSMAN. Words make people disappear. And that's what I did. I made him disappear.

> (*They're both quiet.* **TAMER** *is unsure what to say. So he just holds* **OSMAN** *until he calms down.* **TAMER** *then takes out a bottle of water from his rucksack and offers it to him.*)

Thank you.

I'm so sorry about this.

I'm not... I'm not usually like this.

TAMER. Not usually drunk?

OSMAN. Not this drunk. Not this drunk in a sports shop.

TAMER. It's an intense time.

OSMAN. It is.

TAMER. And for some reason it seems like no one is working here so... you know, cry away.

OSMAN. Why would anyone be working on this floor? Who would steal skis?

TAMER. That's true.

OSMAN. So... why are you buying a raft?

TAMER. I ... I just wanted to see if I could get to Cyprus or I don't know, Italy?

OSMAN. In a raft?

TAMER. Why not?

OSMAN. Are you a smuggler?

TAMER. Oh I don't do drugs.

OSMAN. People.

TAMER. What?

OSMAN. Are you a people smuggler?

TAMER. Me? No.

OSMAN. Are you trying to run away?

TAMER. Run away?

OSMAN. The sea is one way to go.

TAMER. Do you think?

OSMAN. I don't think anyone can run away from Egypt.

TAMER. No?

OSMAN. You will always be found.

TAMER. You think?

OSMAN. I hope.

>   *(They're quiet for a moment.)*

Sharm El Sheikh.

TAMER. What?

OSMAN. Try to find where the resorts buy their rafts. Where they get all their water things for tourists. Banana boats and all that. Those shops will have a raft that can take you to Cyprus.

TAMER. That's a good idea.

OSMAN. And good luck.

Good luck with your raft.

TAMER. Thank you.

I hope you feel better soon.

I know things feel... impossible.

But it can't stay like that forever.

OSMAN. I hope so.

Scene Twenty One

(**TAMER** *is attempting to inflate a plastic raft with a manual pump, on a deserted beach,* **ALIA** *is there as well.*)

TAMER. This shouldn't take too long.

ALIA. It's been hours.

TAMER. Well, it's a big raft, I got the best one, I wanted it... us to be comfortable.

ALIA. I think that maybe this is a sign.

(*He stops.*)

TAMER. A sign?

ALIA. You know? Like God telling us this is a really bad idea?

TAMER. Which God? Yours or mine?

ALIA. Tamer I'm serious!

TAMER. Alia, please.

ALIA. Tell me again why we're doing this.

TAMER. Because we want to be together.

ALIA. No, I'm serious, read me the list.

TAMER. If we're gonna catch the tide then I can't stop.

ALIA. Please. Please read me the list again.

(**TAMER** *stops, looks at her, gives in.*)

TAMER. OK fine.

(*Gets the list out.*)

Reason number 1. Cairo is shit.

Reason number 2. We're in love.

Reason number 3. Your father can and probably will kill me.

Reason number 4. You no longer have a hymen.

ALIA. ...

That's it? I mean, I love you, but I don't know if I'm willing to *die* for you.

TAMER. Should I repeat number three to you? Because I'm starting to feel that perhaps we don't quite feel the same way about each other.

ALIA. My father can kill you, but that doesn't mean he will.

TAMER. You're right. He'll just get one of his henchmen to do it.

ALIA. Stop saying stuff like that.

TAMER. I'm not the one that brought up dying here.

ALIA. He wouldn't. He wouldn't just kill you.

TAMER. So say your father has noticed that some... guy has taken his only daughter –

ALIA. You didn't take me.

TAMER. – away to the fucking north coast, in order to put her on a boat –

ALIA. Raft.

TAMER. – and risk her life to get her to Italy. Let's say he hasn't found out you're missing by now and we go back. Can you guarantee that your father will not find a way for me to stay the fuck away from you? Permanently?

ALIA. Stop swearing.

TAMER. Answer the question Alia.

ALIA. ...

(He starts pumping again.)

TAMER. Exactly.

ALIA. I didn't even answer!

TAMER. This is crazy! You're the one who came up with this plan!

ALIA. I know. I just... It seemed like a good idea at the time. Now it just seems a bit, I don't know, dangerous.

(He stops.)

TAMER. And you only realized this now?? You decide to have these doubts after the trip to Alexandria, and the ride here, and NOW you decide to tell me that maybe this isn't such a good idea? Fuck Alia!

ALIA. Calm down Tamer, I'm just –

(He starts pumping furiously.)

TAMER. You always do this.

ALIA. What do you mean? I always do what?

TAMER. Change your mind. You want to do something and then suddenly you don't.

ALIA. What?

TAMER. You want to get out of Cairo for the day then you don't. You want to break up with me then you don't. You want to see me so I take an hour to get to your side of town then you say you can't see me –

ALIA. Can you hear yourself –

TAMER. You want to make out, then you don't –

ALIA. It's not an easy –

TAMER. – and now YOU came up with the plan to run away to Cyprus or Italy or whatever using a raft, I said let's save up for visas, you're the one that said we'll never be able to get visas, that we definitely won't be able to do it without your father knowing, and now you've changed your mind!

ALIA. I haven't changed my mind!

TAMER. Whatever Alia. You do what you like. I'm going to go with or without you.

> *(She stares at him. He's focused on inflating the raft.)*

ALIA. You're going with or without me?

TAMER. Yes.

ALIA. I knew it. I knew it all along. You were just using me.

TAMER. What?

ALIA. You just wanted me so you can get the money to buy this stupid boat –

TAMER. Raft.

ALIA. – just so you can afford to go without having to pay those, those smugglers! You did all this just so you can go to Italy and be European and have anal sex with all the Italian girls!

> *(He stops.)*

TAMER. Anal sex? Why are you talking about anal sex right now?!

ALIA. You know very well why!

TAMER. I just asked once Alia, it doesn't –

ALIA. Do you think it's easy for me? To be… to be… sexual? To be here right now? To be in love with you? I hate it! I hate being in love with you. I hate it because I'm standing here right now, and it's pitch black and I'm terrified of the sea, and I have no idea what the fuck

I am doing, and I would rather be here now than live without you. And that terrifies me. And I don't want to reach the other side and lose you. Just because I don't want to have anal sex.

TAMER. ...

I want to be with you Alia. I don't care about... that.

ALIA. You say that now –

TAMER. I'm here too Alia.

THE CITY. Lina didn't see the signs the night her brother left.

> *(He kisses her.)*

ALIA. I'm sorry. I got scared.

THE CITY. You would think when a family member disappears you would notice.

You would feel something is wrong.

> *(She kisses him.)*

TAMER. It's ok, I'm scared too.

> *(He kisses her.)*

THE CITY. Lina didn't. She came home, calmed her parents' worry when it began to bubble over.

ALIA. I panicked. You know what I'm like about sex.

> *(She kisses him.)*

THE CITY. Then they realised he had left his phone in his room. Other than that, nothing was out of the ordinary.

TAMER. I know, I'm sorry, I shouldn't have shouted at you.

> *(He kisses her.)*

THE CITY. Lina stuck to the plan for two days, but after they found the phone, she got worried. And she told her parents about Alia.

ALIA. No, you didn't do anything wrong, I started it.

(She kisses him.)

THE CITY. That's when they realised that Alia was also missing. The only clue they had was an entry in a notebook she left.

TAMER. But I should have understood from the beginning –

(They kiss each other.)

ALIA. No, no you reacted perfectly norm –

TAMER. No, I'm sorry I –

ALIA. I love you.

TAMER. I love you more.

(They kiss.)

THE CITY. It said, 'I love him so much, but there's no space for us here.'

TAMER. It's gonna be OK. We're gonna be ok.

*(**TAMER** continues inflating the raft.)*

THE CITY. These days Lina still thinks about them all the time. Did they manage to get visas? Did they get airline tickets? Did they drive out into the desert to live in isolation? The most popular story in her head is that they sailed to Italy, where they are living now, eating lots of pizza and wearing skimpy outfits. Kissing in the street.

She likes to imagine she'll receive a postcard, "Greetings from Italia!"

And he'll tell her he's fine, that he's living in Rome.

He'll tell her about how he and Alia barely survived, rescued by a cargo ship. She'll find out how they struggled to survive in Naples together, working odd jobs for very little pay, how they learned Italian bit by bit, by watching dubbed films and listening to Italian music.

Then he'll tell her how Alia's family don't talk to her anymore, how she has nephews and nieces that don't know about their aunt who ran away to Italy in her twenties.

LINA. That's my favourite version of what could have happened.

And I know it's silly. I know it has nothing to do with reality. But in those moments when that gnawing, empty feeling of not knowing overwhelms me, I think of that story.

Of a beach in the north coast. And a raft. And a silly fight they must have had because that's what people in love are like.

THE CITY. And it's not the only version.

LINA. Sometimes they land in Italy, sometimes in Greece, sometimes in Cyprus, once they were in Malta, and sometimes they don't go to Europe at all. Sometimes they spend the rest of their lives together and sometimes they don't.

THE CITY. But they're happy.

LINA. Always.

Always in my stories, they're happy.

Scene Twenty Two

(The Dokki flat. **OSMAN** *is in the flat with* **MAYA**.*)*

MAYA. You're getting married.

OSMAN. What?

MAYA. Zeina's pregnant.

OSMAN. Maya, stop.

MAYA. So what is it?

OSMAN. She left me.

MAYA. What? I'm so sorry, I didn't know.

OSMAN. It's fine. It happens.

MAYA. Still shit though.

OSMAN. That's not why I wanted to talk to you. I need to tell you something.

MAYA. OK...

OSMAN. I just wanted to say...

MAYA. You're worrying me, what's going on?

OSMAN. I'm sorry.

I'm so sorry, Maya.

MAYA. Osman no.

OSMAN. I'm so sorry for letting you down, for letting everyone down and putting all our lives in danger.

MAYA. What are you talking about?

OSMAN. I'm sorry for everything. I fucked everything up and –

MAYA. Stop. Stop this right now.

OSMAN. I just –

MAYA. No. Stop blaming yourself.

Look, I'm only going to say this once so you better listen carefully.

OSMAN. ...

MAYA. I am proud of you. I am so proud of everything you've done. I am proud of the fight you've put up, and I am so proud of being your sister.

OSMAN. Really?

MAYA. Really.

OSMAN. I don't deserve –

MAYA. It doesn't matter, does it? This is exactly how I feel.

I wouldn't be who I am today if it wasn't for you, do you realise that?

OSMAN. I ... I don't know what to say.

MAYA. You don't need to say anything. Just give me a hug already!

*(They hug. **MAYA**'s phone buzzes. She plays a voice note. It's **LINA**.)*

VOICE NOTE. Heyyy, I'm downstairs in the car. Parking's a bitch, I haven't been able to find a spot so come find me when you're done.

*(**MAYA**' is a bit torn.)*

OSMAN. Go go.

MAYA. You sure? I can tell her to keep looking.

OSMAN. I'm going to be fine. Go to Lina, send her my love.

MAYA. Will do. See you next week.

(**MAYA** *leaves.* **OSMAN** *stands listlessly. He then opens his laptop and tentatively starts to write.*)

OSMAN. These are my last words.

At least for a while. I've decided to give up writing entirely. Hopefully I will give up thinking in the process as well.

It's been years now...

Years since you've... disappeared. Since you've left. Since you've gone missing.

You'll be shocked to know that I've made the decision to leave. Canada. I still haven't been able to tell anyone. So here I am telling you first. I've already started the immigration process.

(**THE CITY** *appears around him.*)

I'm not sure I'm ready. I'm not ready to live in the cold. I'm not ready to be an exile. Maybe that's why I want Maya to come with me. Maybe I'm just a selfish bastard as always.

I don't know if I will be able to convince her though.

Only Cairo, eh? Only Cairo will push you to your absolute limits and then suddenly...you're in love. You're in love and you're entangled and stuck. How does this city do that? How do you do that?

THE CITY. ...

OSMAN. My sister is so much braver than me. So much wiser as well. She's going to be OK, right?

THE CITY. ...

OSMAN. Maybe it's better for me to leave. Maybe it's better to leave it to the brave and to the wise. I unfortunately am neither.

I'm a ghost. One of the many. One of the undead. Just like you said. Just like this city.

I want to wait for your return. I want to believe you're out there. I want to believe you got away. I want to believe that maybe, one day, by the time you return we will be dancing at Maya and Lina's wedding. In a new era. We will dance. Totally and utterly free.

Like we used to dream of.

> (**MAYA** *and* **LINA** *appear. They start to dance in their own imaginary wedding. They dance to something cheesy and 80's and Arabic, like a song in the style of Dalida's* **["HELWA YA BALADY"]**.)

Maybe one day.

THE CITY. The revolution lives on comrade.

In our hearts.

In our minds.

In our fragments.

In our ghosts.

OSMAN. In our motherfucking bodies.

THE CITY. Always.

> (**OSMAN** *looks at what he wrote, he deletes it and closes his laptop.*)

> (*The girls continue dancing.* **OSMAN** *looks at them. Maybe they look like an older version of the time they first danced together. Was it Justin Bieber? Or Taylor Swift?* **OSMAN** *joins* **THE CITY**. *They all watch the girls dance. Tension builds. It feels like 'that moment' in Tahrir, when everything stopped for a split second, where everyone held their breath,*

where everything was about to change for the better, but nothing other than the two girls dancing is happening. They are in their own world. **THE CITY** *watches them. Like ghosts.)*

(The girls stop dancing. They look at **THE CITY** *staring at them. They look at the audience staring at them.)*

(Blackout.)

End

Lightning Source UK Ltd.
Milton Keynes UK
UKHW020612210223
417373UK00010B/234